Not Well Advised

NOT WELL ADVISED

PETER SZANTON

NEW YORK

Russell Sage Foundation AND *The Ford Foundation*

PUBLICATIONS OF RUSSELL SAGE FOUNDATION

Russell Sage Foundation was established in 1907 by Mrs. Margaret Olivia Sage for the improvement of social and living conditions in the United States. In carrying out its purposes, the Foundation conducts research under the direction of members of the staff or outside scholars, in the general fields of social science and public policy. As an integral part of its operation, the Foundation from time to time publishes books or pamphlets resulting from these activities. Publication under the imprint of the Foundation does not necessarily imply agreement by the Foundation, its Trustees, or its staff with the interpretations or conclusions of the authors.

THE FORD FOUNDATION

The Ford Foundation is a private nonprofit institution dedicated to the public well being. It seeks to identify and contribute to the solution of problems of national or international importance. The Foundation works mainly by granting funds to institutions, organizations, and individuals for experimental, demonstration, and developmental efforts that give promise of producing advances in various fields. The Foundation was established in 1936 by Henry Ford and Edsel Ford. It became a national organization in 1950.

Library of Congress Catalog Number: 80-69174

Standard Book Number: 0-87154-874-7

For Carol

CONTENTS

PREFACE

This is a book about advice—especially advice to local public officials. It tries to determine why analyses and proposals offered to local public agencies by consultants of many kinds so often seem to be useless, or at least go unused. The book offers an answer to that question and then suggests a number of ground rules—for advisers, consumers of advice, and third-party funders of advice—that I believe would improve matters.

It began, however, as a book about universities, and its form and emphasis reflect that origin. Its source was a request from officers of the Ford Foundation, in 1976, that I assess the results of the Foundation's considerable effort in the 1950s and 1960s to help provoke and support useful university responses to urban problems, especially by the provision of research and analysis.

For the previous twenty years, and especially during the late 1960s and early 1970s when the "urban crisis" loomed large in the national consciousness, American universities had been regarded as potentially rich sources of useful advice to municipal governments. And pressed to prove "relevant," or to find new sources of financial support, or to utilize the city as a laboratory, or simply to respond to the genuine needs of the troubled communities around them, academics attempted to provide such advice.

The attempt took many forms. In some cases the universities responded as institutions, establishing centers or schools of urban affairs intended, in part, to design and in some cases even to help introduce more rational policy or more effective programs. In other instances, individual professors or instructors, generally with federal or foundation funding, set to work on concrete problems of real or imagined importance to the local government. Some advice was addressed to mayors, some to low-level operating officials, much to no identifiable client. The subject of some was well specified, more was vague. Some was rooted in an established discipline or, more rarely, drew on several disciplines; more displayed little discipline or none.

That diverse history produced a very wide range of results. But whatever its intellectual merits, strikingly little of the advice generated by academics had the intended effect—or any effect—on cities. Indeed, the larger, more institutional and more ambitious the effort, the less effect it appeared to have. The effort as a whole has therefore been generally accounted a failure.

The reasons for this failure, moreover, have been thought to be fairly clear: the academy, concerned with general principles rather than specific situations, valuing originality of insight above utility of conclusion, distracted by the requirements of teaching and basic research and seeking the approval of academic peers rather than municipal clients, was simply an unsuitable setting for the production of timely, specific and practical advice, and for casting it in terms city officials could absorb.

Reviewing the history of university-based attempts to advise municipal agencies, this book finds the evaluation of that experience as a failure to be oversimple but not wrong. The book goes on to argue, however, that the asserted causes of that failure, while plausible, are so far from being the whole truth, or even the main truth, as to be grossly misleading. It suggests that, disadvantageous as they were, the characteristics of the academic world cannot fully explain the frequent inability of academics to provide useful advice to urban officials since such failure was an outcome typical not only of university-based efforts to advise city governments, but of the work of a wide variety of non-academic providers of advice—not-for-profit research corporations, management consulting firms, and the analytic staffs of manufacturers, for example. Academics, moreover, seem to have been able to provide advice of far greater value to other clients. A far better explanation is that city governments are particularly weak and constrained users of any advice, and are sharply limited in their capacity to act on recommendations for change. It is from that proposition that the book derives its concluding suggestions to would-be producers, consumers, and third-party funders of advice about how matters might be improved.

The breadth of the subject precluded any fully comprehensive review of the advice provided to American cities, even by universities. Instead I have absorbed the available accounts, drawn on my own experience with New York City's intensive effort to elicit advice from many sources, and have amplified that background by brief, first-hand examinations of advising relationships in six other U.S. cities. The result is hardly encyclopedic. It undoubtedly fails to report many notable relationships of adviser and advised. Nor does it employ a close-grained typology of advising relationships or very sensitive measures of their degrees of success. The study is therefore partial in coverage and crude in method. Nonetheless, it reaches conclusions that a considerable body of evidence seems to support and that correspond to the educated instincts of the most skillful practitioners of consulting and of local government. I have therefore stated both my conclusions and the lessons that seem to me to flow from them in plain and unreserved form. This is not because I imagine that they represent demonstrated truth, but for two other reasons: I believe that, if observed, these lessons would improve much current practice; and whether observed or not, their formulation in stark terms may stimulate, in the small community of those interested, useful reflection and debate.

Acknowledgments

As in any such enterprise, the author's debts are large and numerous. William Pendleton of the Ford Foundation first proposed that I undertake this work; he patiently pressed for its completion, and, as an acute and early critic of the relationships I describe, introduced me to many of the home truths of the field.

Researchers, consultants, and city officials, too numerous to name, were remarkably generous with their time and candor in describing their own roles in the relationships this book describes. Graham Allison, David Grossman, Edward Hamilton, Frederick Hayes, Norman Krumholz, Wesley Posvar, Arnold Shore, Donald Stokes, and Melvin Webber set aside their own work long enough to review the initial manuscript, noting errors, questioning enthusiasms, and pointing out holes in the argument. Bernard Gifford generously proposed that the Russell Sage Foundation support a revision and updating of the manuscript. Carolyn Szanton repeatedly corrected its prose, John Purcell provided helpful supplementary research, and Hendrikje Becksvoort painstakingly deciphered and cheerfully typed the final results.

Not Well Advised

CHAPTER 1

Where the Action Was

If language is not used accurately, then what is
said is not meant. If what is said is not meant, then
what ought to be done remains undone. . . .
Hence there must be clarity in what is said; that
matters above all.

CONFUCIUS
The Analects, XIII

The "Urban Crisis"

Americans have always worried about their cities. Though
urban centers afforded economic opportunity, cultural diver-
sity, adventure, novelty, and anonymity, cities have been regarded from the opening of our national history as diseased,
debased, confining, and politically dangerous.[1] During the first
half of the twentieth century, however, that historic suspicion
began to diminish. Urban population, 16 percent of the U.S.
total in 1860, had grown to almost 40 percent by 1900. City
voters came to dominate national (though not state) elections,
and their candidates were not notably more demogogic than
those of rural areas. Advances in public health sharply lowered
the incidence of disease in cities. And urban patterns of life no
longer seemed exceptional; they had become the norm.

Dissatisfactions with city life remained, but they were hardly radical. In the 1930s and 1940s overcrowding was the great concern; the "urban problem" of those decades was the miserable housing of the poor. In the 1950s, urban commentary focused on the weakness of land-use planning and on the presumed advantages of metropolitan government.

By 1960, however, more fundamental urban problems had again begun to impinge on the national consciousness. For most major cities, especially the older metropolises of the Northeast and Midwest, a hard three-way squeeze had developed. The demands for services from local government were expanding; city revenues were growing too slowly to meet those demands; and the effective authority of urban officials was diminishing.

Behind the intensifying demand for services lay the growing proportions of the poor, the black, the disadvantaged, and the dependent in urban populations. Their expectations for goods and services were rising, but the movement of upper- and middle-class families to the suburbs, coupled with the traditional dependence of local governments on property taxes, sharply limited city revenues. Faced with the pressure to do more and the necessity to accomplish it with (relatively) less, city governments found it difficult to do anything at all. Their former freedom of action was increasingly limited by municipal employees now more militant and far more fully organized (the number of unionized local government employees doubled between 1960 and 1970) and by newly assertive neighborhood, ethnic, religious, and racial groups. The wisdom that "you can't fight city hall" had been turned on its head. City hall was easy to fight, not hard to stalemate, and even possible to beat.

The result was that American city life, which for fifty years had grown more attractive, more humane, and more prosperous, appeared by the early 1960s to be receding on each of these scales. Though the hard evidence is neither uniform nor complete, it tends to confirm the popular impressions of the time—that at least the large and older cities of the Northeast and Midwest were becoming more repellent, ugly, dirty, and dangerous.

Whether this situation deserved the label "urban crisis" is debatable. Arguably this was no crisis but simply a heightened awareness of classical urban difficulties, measured against raised expectations and magnified by racial tension. Demands on municipal services had increased steadily for decades; in-migration of the poor and jobless had been occurring for two centuries; out-migration of the middle class had been proceeding rapidly since the development of trolley systems at the beginning of the century; and the existence of forceful special interest groups in cities was hardly new. Some urban problems, moreover, were clearly diminishing. Congestion was decreasing, the housing conditions of the poor were improving, public forms of racial discrimination were receding, and the black population was making important economic gains.[2]

The case can also be made, finally, that if a "crisis" existed, it was not urban. Poverty, inadequate social services, and racial tension were all more common outside the major cities than within them.[3] Yet the popular judgment reflected a demonstrable objective truth: many cities were faltering if not failing. Their physical structures were decaying as populations declined. Their economies were weakening as commercial and residential tax bases eroded and jobs disappeared. Their social structures were strained not merely by neighborhood and ethnic and religious division, as before, but now by race—a more evident, more pervasive, and potentially far more explosive distinction. Their politics were growing more embittered. And perhaps most profoundly, cities seemed to be failing in two fundamental social roles. They were no longer effectively socializing in-migrants, and they were no longer adequately employing them.

The Cities Respond

City governments responded to these developments in essentially two ways. Mainly, they sought and expended additional funds. Indeed, expenditures by state and local governments in these years grew at astounding rates. In 1954, state and local government expenditures stood at $30 billion, 8 percent of the nation's GNP; by 1974 they amounted to $206 billion, almost 15 percent of GNP.* During the same period, while federal employment rose from 2.2 to 2.7 million, or 23 percent, state and local government employment rose from 4.6 to 11.6 million, or 125 percent.[4] Local government expenditures on housing and urban renewal increased more than five times in those two decades; on health and hospitals and on police and fire protection more than six times; on education more than seven; and on welfare more than eight.[5]

Strikingly, the rate of growth in these expenditures was higher for major cities than for state and local government generally. Though inconsistencies in the data and shifts in financing responsibilities make these expenditures hard to compare, one careful study has concluded that in the decade 1962–1972, while all state and local expenditures grew by 163 percent, those of a representative sample of twenty-eight large cities grew by 198 percent.[6] Much of this additional expenditure, of course, was absorbed by inflation and by the very large increase in the average earnings of public sector employees, which in those twenty years almost tripled.[7] But virtually every local government function also increased in scope, complexity, and ambition.

The resulting growth in municipal expenditure was financed

*This enormous growth occurred while federal expenditures grew quite modestly —from 19.2 to 21.4 percent of GNP. Indeed, if transfer payments to individuals are excluded, federal expenditures over these years *declined* as a proportion of the GNP.

largely by federal grants. This was the period in which the fiscal relationships of the federal system were being quietly but profoundly transformed, as tens of billions of dollars raised by federal taxation began flowing through state and city budgets. But state and local tax rates also increased sharply. The ratio of local government revenues (excluding federal grants) to personal income rose from under 9 percent in 1954 to over 14 percent in 1974. In cities containing high concentrations of the poor, the proportions were much higher; in New York, for example, it had risen by 1973 to almost 23 percent.[8]

Yet demand for municipal services grew at a greater rate than city incomes. The second general strategy, therefore, was to accomplish more with less. Reform and innovation were to make programs more cost-effective and enhance the efficiency of city government.

This was a policy more often announced than carried out, to be sure, for it encountered political, bureaucratic, and conceptual difficulties of awesome proportions. Local government costs were overwhelmingly personnel costs. Substantial savings therefore required fewer employees, lower salaries, or reduced fringe benefits. Yet, especially in the larger and older cities, the private sector jobs to which city employees might have moved were disappearing, the tradition of the city government as residual (and generous) employer was strong, costly benefit packages had become customary, and expanding municipal bureaucracies deployed formidable voting strength. And the fast-growing public service unions, at odds with agency administrators over everything else, were their determined allies behind one proposition: if budget cuts were unavoidable they must be taken elsewhere; reductions in *this* department would cripple absolutely essential services.

Moreover, it was far from clear how greater efficiency was to be obtained, especially at a time when local community interests in greater "responsiveness" posed still another competing claim. The outlines of at least four largely inconsistent approaches to more effective local government had begun to emerge: the *integration* of traditional departments and agencies into large "super departments"; the *decentralization* of operating control and management discretion to administrators at borough, ward, or district levels; *control* (or influence) *by local communities* and neighborhoods themselves; and *"privatization,"* the devolution into private hands of responsibility for services which, like trash collection, seemed more efficiently performed in the commercial marketplace.

The search for greater cost-effectiveness proceeded in two directions: toward more productive technology (computer-controlled traffic signals, high-pressure trash compactors); and toward new planning, policy-making, or management methods (systems analysis, program budgeting). And since local officials knew that industry, the professional consulting firms, and the federal government all had greater experience with such innovations than they did, they sought help from each of those sources. Mayors and department heads pressed local industries to volunteer experts in efficiency studies, management effectiveness, accounting methods. The management consulting industry was employed by city governments for the first time in significant degree. Federal officials experienced in the new planning and management procedures were hired away from Washington.

And encouraged by foundation and federal agencies, some local officials looked to the universities as well for help. They found a number of academics and university administrators eager to respond. The cities, bedeviled by problems, stood awaiting help; the universities, rich in understanding, were obliged to provide it. In doing so, the universities would deepen their own knowledge of the life and society around them. So, at least, went the rhetoric of the time. In his inaugural address as president of the University of Cincinnati,

Warren Bennis expressed the conviction in characteristically expansive terms.

> A generation ago, Washington was the power center where young men could work the levers that had an impact on the world. Today, City Hall is where the action is and the city itself is the focus of all the major problems. . . . Properly, the universities should be, along with City Hall, the command post of all the operations to reclaim, renew, rebuild and revitalize the city. . . . The city around us is itself a university without walls.[9]

The 1960s, especially the early 1960s, were a time of great confidence in "problem solving" and great acceptance of the "action-intellectual," a period of easy relations between decision makers and scholars. And "If it was possible to go to the moon" then anything was possible, given only the requisite will and funding. It was a time in which scholarship leaned to the empirical and bent to the "relevant." That a body of usable "urban" knowledge existed in the academy was generally assumed; that its existence created an obligation to help solve the cities' problems was widely asserted.

Two disciplines, public administration and city planning, to be sure, had long concerned themselves with city government. But neither was now in favor. For one thing, both had tended to divorce themselves from politics, and politics now was recognized as the matrix in which governmental action took place. For another, their perspectives seemed too limited. The problems of the cities were only partially administrative or aesthetic; they were technical, economic, demographic, social, moral, and all of these together. The hope, therefore, was that a far wider variety of scholarly skills and perspectives might be brought to bear.

The analogy often employed was that of rural extension. Through agricultural experiment stations and the county-agent system America's land-grant universities had for eighty years led the striking advance in farm technology and enriched the lives of rural families. Why could not urban universities, operating "urban observatories" and employing "urban extension agents," help solve the complex problems of America's cities? In retrospect, the question seems substantive and difficult.* In the 1960s, however, it sounded simply rhetorical. Why not indeed? There seemed every reason to believe that the university itself would be enriched by the attempt. The city would become its laboratory, a source of problems for advanced students and idealistic faculty to attack, a provider of new revenues, an anchor in the real world, and a source of opportunities to generate data, refine hypotheses, and advance social understanding. The universities might thus meet the social responsibilities now being widely assigned to them. And the cities might, over time, be transformed.

The Academic Company

The universities to which American cities looked for help (and to which foundations and federal agencies looked on cities' behalf) were diverse in history, purpose, and clientele. Of the roughly 2,400 U.S. institutions of higher education accredited in the mid-1960s, some 160 were true universities. These fell into several categories.

The prestigious private eastern universities had evolved from the colonial colleges of liberal arts. Transformed by exposure to German scholarship in the nineteenth century, they con-

---

*As has since been recognized, the rural extension analogy was faulty on several grounds. Rural extension developed slowly and experimentally over half a century; it was limited and well specified in purpose; and it was rooted in a congruence of values between the researchers and the whole constituency on which their schools depended. None of these conditions held with respect to urban problems.

sisted largely of research-oriented graduate schools on the German model superimposed on liberal arts teaching colleges of English tradition. Harvard, Yale, and Columbia typified the class. A second and closely related category comprised the small group of private universities—Johns Hopkins, Stanford, and the University of Chicago principal among them—established in the late nineteenth century entirely on the German model. Like the schools in the first group, they were devoted to teaching and research of high quality and lacked any substantial tradition of local public service. A third set was composed of the older state universities—those of Michigan, Minnesota, Wisconsin, and California, for example. These were oriented both by doctrine and the exigencies of tax support toward public service as well as research and teaching, but their reputations and student bodies were national, and their academic goals took precedence. A fourth and rapidly growing category was composed of new state-supported universities evolving from the smaller land-grant, agricultural and mechanical, and teachers colleges. Typically, these schools served local and vocationally-oriented students, many of whom attended part time. And public service had been one of their explicit, if loosely defined, objectives since the Morrill Act of 1862. Finally, there were two local public universities supported directly by city governments—the City University of New York and the University of Cincinnati—which, like Temple University in Philadelphia, had been established in the nineteenth century to serve the aspiring urban poor.

Differing as these universities did in academic standards, in sources of funding, in degree of devotion to service as against teaching or research, in the capacities, ages and economic status of their student bodies, and in their concern for their immediate communities, they nonetheless had much in common. One link was that all had been part of an enormous expansion in American higher education, and almost all had been made vulnerable by it. There were twenty times as many undergraduates enrolled in 1966 as in 1900, and more than one hundred times the number of graduate students. Much of this growth, moreover, had occurred in the 1950s and early 1960s; the roughly 5.5 million American undergraduates and 650,000 graduate students of 1966 outnumbered their 1950 counterparts by almost three to one. Enrollment in public institutions had grown particularly fast, from exactly half of total enrollment in the late 1930s to almost two-thirds of the very much larger number enrolled in the late 1960s. The larger universities had become huge. Harvard, Yale, and the Universities of Michigan and Minnesota, for example, each had enrolled between 300 and 650 students in the 1870s; they now ranged in size from 10,000 to more than 40,000 students.[10] Budgets were similarly swollen; Columbia's, $20 million in 1953, was $120 million in 1966.[11] And together with salaries in the not-for-profit sector generally, academic pay in this period had advanced very rapidly; genteel poverty was no longer accepted as the necessary circumstance of scholars.

The result was that by the early 1960s, many U. S. universities were financially vulnerable. They were larger, more complex, and harder to manage than before; responsible for huge payrolls and dramatically expanded physical plants; and undercapitalized and dependent on continued growth in revenues. But in the middle 1960s enrollment growth began to taper off just as federal research funding started to decline. Inflation compounded the problem, and by 1968 a Carnegie Corporation study found that 71 percent of a representative group of universities was either already in financial difficulty or was clearly headed for it.[12] Though private universities had come under greater pressure than public ones, all types of institutions were affected. As a result, by the late 1960s most universities were actively seeking new sources of funds.

A second characteristic common to virtually all American

universities was that they were deeply influenced by the social concerns of the day. As Abraham Flexner had noted in 1930, American universities existed "not outside but inside the general social fabric of a given era. . . . They are not something apart, something historic, something that yields as little as possible to forces and influences that are more or less new. They are, on the contrary . . . an expression of the age. . . ."[13] In the nineteenth century, those external forces had created schools of agriculture, engineering, home economics, business administration—fields of scholarship then unknown in Germany or England. They had induced the universities to serve the children of farmers and workers, to create agricultural experiment stations and service bureaus, and to acknowledge that, in the United States, the role of universities was neither to form gentlemen nor to train only scholars, lawyers, doctors, and divines. It was to produce more skillful engineers, more productive farmers, more competent businessmen, a more prosperous nation. Jacques Barzun put the point broadly: "The American university is a residual institution—asked to do whatever individuals or society cannot do for themselves."[14] By the 1960s, what universities were being asked to do—by mayors, editorialists, foundations, entrepreneurial or socially-conscious faculty, and by their own student bodies—was to take up a position on the urban battlefront.

But it was also typical of American universities that, though more deeply affected by the social currents of the day than most of their European counterparts, they were not urban in spirit or history. All of the great continental universities had developed in cities. Most American colleges and universities had been set in rural areas or small towns. As Clark Kerr wrote in 1968:

. . . the religious denominations that started most of the early colleges preferred rural sites as more fitting and particularly more moral locations; the land grant movement had a rural basis; boosters of new towns, as the population moved west, boosted local colleges. Many of the colleges and universities now in urban locations were once in the outskirts of the city, and saw it grow up around them, often with the greatest regret. . . . Except for occasional studies, as at the University of Chicago in the 1930s, and occasional institutions, as at Berkeley and Syracuse, the city was largely ignored.[15]

The result was that most American universities had little working experience with the problems of urban government and little contact with the officials whose profession it was to deal with those problems. Indeed, much of what contact they had was painful. The great postwar expansion of universities had created problems of parking, housing,* local tax-loss and town-gown relations that steadily irritated the relations of many local officials and university administrators.

Another characteristic shared by American universities was that they were organized almost entirely into departments defined by single academic disciplines—economics, physics, biology, romance languages. It was the department and not deans or university presidents that decided on hiring, tenure, and promotion (a fact that mayors and municipal department heads were slow to understand). And the dominant loyalties of faculty members attached not so much to the university (and still less to the local community in which the university happened to be set) as to the department and the national and international community of scholars of which it was part. It was to the discipline's national organization that scholars looked for recognition; to the discipline's journal that they looked for publication; in the discipline's departments in other schools that they sought to place their students. Organization by discipline is a powerful motivator of methodological prog-

---

*Interestingly, the first three rent-control systems in the United States after World War II were adopted in university-dominated towns: Ann Arbor, Cambridge, Berkeley.

ress, specialized research, and informed teaching. But it is a poor framework for applying interdisciplinary and nondisciplinary knowledge to the poorly defined, highly ramified, politically charged problems of local government.

Finally, as they sought to engage themselves in the understanding and solution of urban problems, universities shared two sources of confusion and disorientation. The first was that the category "urban problems," meaning everything, meant nothing. What was to be addressed: racial conflict, unemployment, housing deterioration, the flight of the middle class, the inadequacies of public transportation, schooling deficiencies, crime, air pollution, the welfare burden? All of these? The dynamics of American cities were—as they still are—only dimly understood. Which of those problems were causes and which effects? Which might yield most readily to analysis? To governmental intervention? Which most seriously threatened the quality of urban life or the governability of metropolitan centers? No one knew.

That uncertainty was compounded by another. City budgets were strained, and city agencies were unaccustomed to supporting research. By and large, therefore, early university efforts to involve themselves in urban issues were funded by third parties—foundations and various agencies of the federal government. The result was confusion not only about what issues should be addressed but about who the client was. Was it the city government—and if so, who in it: the mayor, the city council, a political appointee heading an agency, or the technicians or bureaucrats who reported to him? Was it an aggrieved ethnic or racial group or neighborhood association? Was it some self-derived conception of the general interest? Or the foundation or federal agency? These questions, too, often had no clear answer. Indeed, once funding was secured, they were seldom asked.

Nonetheless, the pull of evident urban needs, the push towards "relevance," the requirement to generate new revenues, and the fact that, immovably fixed in deteriorating urban settings, many universities had a substantial stake in the fate of their own cities were pressures too powerful to ignore. Curricular reforms were undertaken, with courses and advanced degree programs developed on urban issues. Training programs for city employees, especially for police and correctional officers, were established. Remedial courses were designed for poorly prepared entering students. The athletic and medical facilities at some schools were opened to neighborhood residents. Universities in decaying areas became active backers of redevelopment. On a quite different plane, university-based scholars contributed greatly to the analysis of local and national issues of social policy and to the design of federal initiatives affecting cities and the poor. The Family Assistance Plan and the Model Cities concept are obvious examples.

These were substantial activities, and any attempt to assess in the large the response of universities to the problems of the cities would have to consider them with care. But our purpose here is far more limited. It is to understand the nature, extent, and typical outcome of university-based attempts to provide useful advice to city officials. Specifying problems, identifying causes, suggesting solutions—these seemed the overriding new tasks set for the academic community by the urban crisis. And they were the tasks whose attempted performance shed most light on the barriers to innovation in local government, on the difficult conditions effective advisers must meet, and on the particular strengths and weaknesses that academics bring to a challenge—not merely speaking truth to power, but influencing power through truth—whose importance is likely to grow.

CHAPTER 2

Attempts to Advise

It must be understood that the children of light
are foolish not merely because they underestimate the power of self-interest among the children of darkness. They underestimate this power
among themselves.

REINHOLD NIEBUHR
The Children of Light and the Children of Darkness

The academic community attempted to advise and inform
urban officials through many mechanisms, but three main in-
struments are worth distinguishing: urban "centers" or "institutes" within universities; federally-funded efforts to induce
urban innovation; and direct and essentially personal consulting of academics with local officials.

The Urban Research Centers

The Urban Institute's 1969 directory of university urban research centers noted that "such centers in the early 1960s
numbered only about two dozen. In 1967, there were about 80.
Today we identify close to 200." The 1971 directory showed

some 300 such centers—roughly twice the number of American universities.[1]

There was much less here than met the eye. The centers typically characterized as "urban" a bewildering miscellany of activities and interests. They held themselves out as sources of teaching and research on the poor, the troubled, the disadvantaged, the unemployed, the aged, the young, and an endless variety of substantive issues from the visual arts through economic development and court reform to pollution control. Diffuseness was not their sole weakness. Especially in their early years, the principal task of most such centers was either to attempt to coordinate "urban related" work in the standard academic departments or to attract external funding. Few possessed the power to hire teachers or researchers or to promote or fire those hired by the departments. They had neither leverage nor prestige within the universities and well deserved the treatment accorded in a satirical 1970 article in *Science:*

> Q: Specifically, what are some of the examples of the Center's work?
> A: Well, the Center staff members have resolved the conflict between teaching and research.
> Q: How?
> A: By doing neither.[2]

Moreover, where the work of these centers had substance, it was far more likely to consist of familiar forms of research and teaching than of advising city government or conducting studies with clear policy relevance. The Center for Metropolitan Planning and Research at Johns Hopkins University, for example, reporting to the Ford Foundation in 1974 on the prior five years of its urban affairs program, described its research activities in twenty-six pages, its education and training work in fourteen, and its "community services"—of which work with local government was one part—in three and one-half.[3] The allocation of effort that breakdown suggests was common. It was also wholly legitimate, of course. Indeed the argument is strong that research and teaching are the only proper functions of universities and the only tasks at which they have a comparative advantage. The point here is simply that even where, as at Johns Hopkins, genuine intellectual effort took place at the "urban centers," little of it consisted of analysis performed for a local decision maker.*

It was characteristic of these centers, moreover, that when they did perform applied work for an urban client, the client was often not a government but a neighborhood or ethnic or racial group—an entity often in conflict with local agencies. This was a period in which many intellectuals regarded city hall less as the instrument of solutions than as the source of problems. City bureaucracies were widely viewed as unresponsive, incompetent, corrupt, or all three; and many action-oriented academics, like activist citizens generally, sympathized with the emerging representatives of the underprivileged. Work for such nongovernmental clients was particularly common at newer schools with large black student populations (Texas Southern University in Houston, for example) where research and policy centers tended naturally to become advocates of views that teachers and students regarded as underrepresented.

There were additional characteristics of urban centers that limited their utility to local governments. One was that when they sought to serve the needs of government at all, many, especially those of the more nationally oriented universities, focused on problems of federal, regional, or state policy. The work of the Harvard–MIT Joint Center is a fair example.

---

*Universities were capable of absorbing "urban" funding in ways that produced far less interest to local decision makers. Early in the 1960s the University of Illinois, for example, received $125,000 from the Ford Foundation's "Urban Extension" program, in part to help "define its urban role." Having expended the money, the university concluded that its proper urban role was simply to continue its "regular teaching and research function."[4]

Another limitation was that even that small proportion of work done for city governments was usually funded by third parties —typically the Ford Foundation, the federal Departments of Housing and Urban Development or of Health, Education and Welfare, or the National Science Foundation. Those funds normally went directly to the universities, not to or through the intended beneficiaries. The universities thus had little incentive to determine what help city agencies wanted or were capable of using. They tended rather to address issues they or their funders regarded as important, attempting only afterwards—often clumsily—to interest city officials in the results.

But the main point is not that the analyses of urban issues performed at universities were irrelevant or unimportant to local officials; it is that so few such analyses were performed. A review in 1967 by the Higher Education Council on urban affairs activities in the Baltimore area, for example, showed twenty of that region's twenty-four institutions of higher education reporting some "urban affairs activities." But none reported attempts to provide advice to any level of local government.[5] Frederick O'R. Hayes and John E. Rasmussen, in a 1972 survey of centers of external advice for cities and states, could not find a single significant case of a university-based institution devoted primarily to serving the research needs of a city or state government.[6]

The available evidence is thin, but it suggests that of the roughly 300 university-based urban centers operating in 1971, not more than 200 engaged in any substantial activity for more than a year; of those, probably more than 150 devoted virtually all their efforts to teaching and to clientless research; and of the remaining 50, a probable majority performed their client-oriented work principally for nongovernmental groups or state and especially federal agencies. Perhaps 10 to 20 centers provided substantial informational or analytic support to a city government; another 20 or 30 may have provided occasional services. But the Hayes-Rasmussen conclusion seems correct: none sought primarily to serve the research needs of local governments.

The National Programs

The various urban centers and institutes represented the most common university responses to pressures for urban relevance, but three national programs provided better tests of the capacity of universities to prove useful to city governments under the stimulus of federal funding.

THE URBAN OBSERVATORIES

The first such program sought to establish a national network of "urban observatories." The observatory notion dated from a 1962 speech of Robert C. Wood, then an MIT political scientist and adviser on urban problems to the federal government, later undersecretary of the Department of Housing and Urban Development. Wood noted that "the study of urban politics lags far behind the natural sciences in the treatment of the phenomena under observation," and that the laboratories and observatories of the natural scientists "with an agreed upon set of tools, an accepted field of observation, a common understanding of the phenomena to be observed . . . build a cumulative record."[7] He argued that a national network of "urban observatories," operated jointly by universities and city governments and following a master research plan, could begin to develop a science of urban affairs.

The talk received considerable notice. Shortly thereafter

Mayor Henry Maier of Milwaukee, then president of the National League of Cities, urged on the federal government the creation of just such a system of observatories to "help us replace our folk knowledge of cities with more scientific knowledge." A group of mayors and university officials endorsed the concept as the beginning of "a new relationship between urban decision makers and the universities."[8] Following discussions among the league, university groups, mayors, and government officials, a six-city Urban Observatory program was begun experimentally, with HUD funding, in June 1968. Six months later, the Office of Education of the Department of Health, Education and Welfare became a joint sponsor (through Title I of the Higher Education Act of 1965), and the number of participating cities expanded to ten: Albuquerque, Atlanta, Baltimore, Kansas City, Milwaukee, Nashville, Boston, Cleveland, Denver, and San Diego.

The program claimed three purposes:

1. To help make available to local governments university resources useful for understanding and solving particular urban and metropolitan problems

2. To achieve a coordinated program of continuing urban research, grounded in practical experience and application, and relevant to the urban management, human resources, and environmental and developmental problems common to a number of regions and communities

3. To advance generally the capacities of universities to relate their research and training activities to urban concerns and to the conditions of urban living

Toward the first objective, the program's guidelines required that in each participating city, policy boards be established and that local officials be well represented on them. The boards were to provide overall guidance, participate in the choice of subjects to be studied, and insure that the work undertaken was relevant and timely to actual municipal decision making. To achieve the second, the National League of Cities, coordinating contractor for the entire program, was instructed to organize the local observatories into a national network. A substantial fraction of the research was to be comparable from city to city so that through parallel studies a body of nationally applicable knowledge would be generated. The third objective, which had depended on Office of Education funds, quickly fell away when Title I funding—tied to educational training and awarded through state agencies—proved difficult to funnel to the observatories.

Two formal and comprehensive evaluations of the observatory program were performed during its life, one by the National Academy of Public Administration in 1971, a second by Greenleigh Associates in 1974. Both were conducted for HUD, and neither had reason to undervalue the program. Both found it of limited utility.

NAPA recommended continuing and expanding the program but found, inter alia, that "organization and administration of the observatories are, in many instances, unsatisfactory . . . little research had been completed to date . . . central leadership and professional direction on national research projects are regarded generally as unsatisfactory."[9]

The Greenleigh study, with a considerably longer history to examine, concluded guardedly that "in 8 out of the 10 local sites . . . the UO did facilitate the utilization of university resources, to a greater or lesser degree among sites. In one of the two remaining sites, it was difficult to make this determination because of conflicting evidence; the other site was determined to have been in jeopardy regarding the achievement of (this) objective from the outset. . . ." With respect to the objectives of the so-called national program, the Greenleigh assessment was that

. . . the concept of a coordinated program of relevant, continuing research in a variety of cities was not realized in its totality. The process of conducting national comparative research was improved over the five-year period, but little headway was made in disseminating the information effectively and efficiently within or without the network system of cities. In the matter of relevance of projects, there is a consensus of opinion that the local-agenda projects were relevant to local problem areas, and that national-agenda projects, because of a breakdown in the dissemination of information were not relevant to individual cities.[10]

Both assessments were probably too generous. It is true that virtually all observatories yielded some useful result. Baltimore, for example, changed its trash-collection procedures along lines suggested by an observatory-sponsored report. Studies of citizen attitudes and of possible social indicators had a wide public readership in San Diego. An analysis of housing inspections in Boston stimulated development of a simpler inspection reporting system and less mechanical use of its findings; "Little City Halls" also were established in response to observatory work. In Albuquerque, the Observatory Board became a useful forum for discussion of various issues between city agencies and among various levels of government, and facilitated informal contacts between administrators wanting help and academics interested in providing it. But overall, the return on the $5 million investment in the observatories was meager. City agencies found the mandatory "national agenda" studies—of citizen participation, municipal finance, government indices, costs of local government services—of little use to them. Their response was to redefine the subjects or to impose changes in research procedure that made results noncomparable with those of other cities. "Local agenda" proposals were bent to suit the research interests and methodological equipment of the academics undertaking them. Participating universities feuded with each other over shares of the funding. City officials had authority over research agendas but lacked the experience or incentive to exercise it; observatory directors, who might have exercised it on their behalf, were typically underfunded, part-time participants. Some underestimated the difficulty of the task; few had the time, the support, or the will to perform it. Some directors, unfamiliar with the universities, sought advice from deans as to staffing the studies. More often than they knew, they were referred not to the professors best qualified, but to those who most needed additional support.

A crude test of the utility of the program as viewed by the cities involved is provided by the response of the participating cities in 1974 when HUD ended its support. Only two of the ten cities were willing to supply sufficient funding of their own to keep the observatories in substantial operation.*

A closer look at two of the observatories, one a representative failure, the other the experiment's clearest success, are revealing.

---

*Of the ten original observatories, those of Denver, Nashville, Albuquerque, Boston, and Milwaukee still exist in one form or another. But aside from the Denver observatory, discussed later, the Nashville observatory is the only substantial institution, with typical annual budgets of roughly half a million dollars, almost all in federal contracts. But the Nashville observatory performs its contract work almost entirely with its own research staff, not with university faculty. The Boston observatory performs specific research projects for the city of Boston but receives only token institutional support from the city. A vestigial Milwaukee observatory is supported by the University.

A second observatory program, involving ten cities with populations under 250,000, was begun in 1975 and was considerably more successful. Although the program is no longer federally funded, eight of the original observatories still exist, and three Indiana cities, not part of the original program, have since entered it. The small city observatories, much more modest in their goals than the original program, vary in the sources of their institutional support (the Bridgeport, Connecticut observatory, for example, is supported by the United Way), but are generally considered useful by city administrations. Interestingly, this program involves no national agenda. It is free of pretensions to developing large urban truths; its projects are modest and well defined in scope (feasible pension reforms, improved street repair procedures, and stray animal control) and tend to be geared to the specific interests of its local supporters.

Cleveland: "A Waste of Time." When the urban observatory program began, Cleveland might reasonably have been picked as a probable success. The troubled city was under pressure to reform and seemed open to innovation. Carl Stokes, its first black mayor, had recruited young and energetic department heads. The city's compact business establishment might have been expected to support rethinking of policies and programs. Of the two universities then interested in participating, one, Case Western Reserve, possessed a strong and potentially useful engineering component. The other, Cleveland State, had a strong urban orientation, a mid-city location, and an almost wholly local student body. But Roy Crawley, president of the National Academy of Public Administration and leader of the NAPA team which evaluated the observatory, found it "a disaster."

Why? The composition of the observatory's board (four agency heads and one middle-level administrator from each of the participating universities) was one difficulty. Though city agencies were well represented, no members were drawn either from the mayor's office or the city council, or the county or state governments. And none of the agency heads on the board regarded the observatory as significant. A larger problem was the absence of a strong director. Managing the relationships among institutions as divergent in values, preoccupations, styles, and objectives as universities and municipal departments, is hard, sensitive, and full-time work. But the specifications for observatory directors were very loosely drawn, and Cleveland's first director was a CSU graduate student with little experience in the city's government.

A first result was that disagreements as to whether studies could be published by their authors held up the observatory's formal establishment for several months, a period during which the attitudes of city officials moved from skepticism to hostility. Control of the observatory then fell by default to the universities, principally to CSU which needed observatory funds to support a struggling Institute of Urban Studies. Since observatory studies offered little promise of academic prestige or advancement, the academics drawn to them were mostly students and junior faculty, largely in the social sciences. Their work proved uneven in quality and maladroit politically. After one highly critical evaluation of Cleveland's Manpower Administration, the head of CSU's Urban Studies program remarked, "No one at Manpower will ever want to work with anyone at the University again." Similarly, a citizen participation study was undertaken without notice to the councilman whose district it examined. Regarding it as a threat, he became a persistent opponent of the observatory.

When the Stokes administration was succeeded by a more traditional regime, control over the observatory shifted to a private university politically allied to the new administration. Nonetheless, little substantive work was undertaken. "This administration has no interest in technical competence. It's a job-distribution enterprise. Representatives of various voting groups are appointed to key jobs and they're trusted because they won't make waves. Why pay good money to hire somebody from a university to find out something damaging?" That was the summary of one informed insider. Agreeing entirely with Crawley's assessment, Norman Krumholz, Cleveland's planning director and a one-time chairman of the observatory's policy board, concluded flatly, "The observatory was a waste of time."[11]

Denver: A Different Story. By all accounts, Denver's experience was different. The observatory there has produced an impressive number of useful reports, including competent studies of municipal finance; the costs of city services; citizen attitudes; housing policy; long-term racial, economic, and demographic trends; public facilities use; and possible forms of metropolitan government. Virtually all its studies were requested by city officials, and a high proportion have affected decision making—some by informing policy debate, some by more directly precipitating action.

A study of Denver's economic base published in 1974, for example, uncovered the beginning of several unfavorable trends. It found that Denver's population growth had essentially ended, and that employment and income growth were falling behind both national and regional rates as newer businesses tended to locate outside the city. The study set the main substantive question for the Denver mayoral campaign of that year. Neither candidate questioned its findings or the significance of those findings; the candidates differed only on which policies could more effectively restimulate the city's economy. The study of public facilities use showed that roughly one-third of the people attending Denver's symphony, museums, and botanic and zoological gardens lived in Colorado but outside Denver, and that finding was promptly used by the city to secure more liberal state support of those facilities. Guidelines produced by the observatory for the deployment of fire-fighting services were adopted by both the city's fire department and budget office.

As a result, the observatory became widely regarded throughout the Denver metropolitan area as a principal source of objective information on issues of local importance. When HUD funding for the nation-wide program ended in 1974, Denver kept its own observatory going, and it does so still. Though most of the observatory's budget is procured through grants and contracts for particular projects, the city provides sufficient institutional support to insure continuity.

Why should Denver's observatory have succeeded when most others failed? We return to that question in the final chapter of this study, but a number of factors are worth noting here. The Denver observatory's Policy Board, unlike Cleveland's, began with representatives of the city council, the regional council of governments and the state government, as well as city agencies. And though the board was evenly divided between educators and city or state officials, of its five academics one was a former state official, one a former councilman and mayor, and two were deeply active in public affairs as private citizens. Its composition, in short, made the board highly sensitive to the environment in which the "consumers" of studies must operate. As was true in Cleveland, all studies produced through the Denver observatory are published. Though drafts are circulated for comment before publication, no change can be made without the permission of the principal investigator. But the subjects for study have been chosen with skill. They have engendered strong public interest (the economic base study), conferred political advantage on the city as a whole (facilities use), reduced costs (fire), and provided data and staff-work impartially to all interested jurisdictions (metropolitan government). No studies have simply evaluated current practice. And virtually all were requested by a public official; the studies have an interested—often a participating—client.

As these facts suggest, leadership of the observatory has been strong and adroit. Its director, F. William Heiss, had spent twelve years in various city agencies before coming to the observatory. He knew most city officials and understood what concerned them. In the observatory's early years, he spent full time directing it. And he personally selected the academics asked to undertake each study. In Denver, studies requested by city officials are undertaken by faculty chosen by the observatory director and selected for a combination of analytic skill and policy sensitivity. (In Cleveland, study proposals generally originated in the universities, and studies approved were conducted by their proponents.) As the head of one of the city's operating departments remarked, "I can go to a guy I know, who knows my problems, and he'll find the professors who may do me some good." There were reciprocal advantages. A faculty member observed, "We wouldn't do this work for the city without the observatory. Bill is doing our marketing."[12]

THE INFORMATION SYSTEMS CONSORTIUM

In the late 1960s, it was often noted that the information available to mayors, administrators, and city council members was generally incomplete and often inaccurate. Local record keeping was disjointed and not standardized; record maintenance was often expensive and inefficient. Though the use of computers had begun to lower costs and improve reliability, logically related information was normally still kept in the separate and noncomparable files of specialized and independent agencies. Fire chiefs observed, for example, that if it were immediately accessible, information on the age, construction, and condition of burning buildings could clearly save lives and property. Typically, the needed data existed, but lay in the separate files or computer memories of city assessors, building inspectors, recorders of deeds, and planning commissions. The information could not be assembled nearly in time to be useful to fire fighters. Less urgent but equally important purposes such as land use planning and tax policy making were just as poorly served. At the same time, businessmen and data-processing firms were asserting that the rudimentary municipal information systems commonly in operation could readily be made far more suitable for day-to-day management purposes.[13]

It was against this background that in 1968 HUD enlisted ten federal departments in an Urban Information Systems Inter-Agency Committee (USAC). Its stated object was ambitious: "to stimulate the development of urban information systems by several orders of magnitude over the past." The following year, USAC sent to each of the 359 U.S. municipalities with populations of between 50,000 and 500,000 a detailed request for proposal (RFP) inviting plans for developing either of two kinds of information systems. One was to be a "subsystem," serving the information requirements of two or more departments with related functions. For example, police, fire, and ambulance services might together use a public safety subsystem. The other was far more comprehensive; it would comprise an "integrated" or total system, providing all major functions of urban government with common or compatible data bases. In each case the system was to be developed by a three-party consortium consisting of the city's government, a commercial electronic data processing firm, and a university or nonacademic research center.

Seventy-nine cities responded and six were eventually chosen. Charlotte, North Carolina and Wichita Falls, Texas were to produce integrated systems; Dayton, Ohio, Long Beach, California, Reading, Pennsylvania, and St. Paul, Minnesota would develop subsystems. As it happened, universities were members of each of the consortia selected.

Over the following five years some $26 million was spent on these projects, more than twice the sum contemplated by the proposals. But the problems of producing the envisioned systems proved vastly more formidable than their sponsors had expected. Only St. Paul dropped from the program prematurely; elsewhere the work continued and, as a result, systems of some utility were developed and useful learning took place. But in no case were original goals even approached.

The experience of the universities in the consortia was uniformly frustrating and unproductive. The difficulty began at the beginning: the RFP had defined no clear role for the universities but suggested three quite different functions: to document progress, to evaluate progress, and to supervise the other participants. The academic entities involved in the consortia varied greatly, including a political science department (the University of Minnesota); interdisciplinary "urban" and "policy studies" institutes (Kansas and California State/Long Beach); a unit composed of faculty from business, education, and planning schools (Dayton); and a state-oriented institute of government (North Carolina), but for each, the choice among functions was unattractive. Few of the university units had the technical capacity for detailed description; all were properly wary of the responsibilities of evaluation; and none possessed either the political authority or the managerial competence to undertake supervision. In all cities, moreover, the work went more slowly and more expensively than either the city governments or the data-processing firms had expected. The governments and data firms therefore sought to limit detailed reporting and to avoid evaluation entirely. Finally, as costs mounted and budgets became tight, the expectable occurred. The universities came to be regarded by their consortium colleagues as dispensable, and in each consortium, university participation diminished over time.

J. Terry Edwards, the director of the University of Kansas's work with the Wichita Falls (Texas) project, has reflected on his experience in terms which speak for all academic participants in the consortia:

One of the continuing confusions of the project was the role of the University. Except for a generalized belief at the initiation of the project that the University participation would be good and the insistence by USAC that a university be involved, there was little thought given to the University's role. Furthermore, within the University there were a number of different actors and participants who had widely divergent interests in the project. For example, the project director had a rather specialized interest in urban geographic information systems. Another participant had a particular interest in organizational change and wanted to participate in the training activities by prompting organizational development (even though the

University had relatively little experience in organizational development at the time) . . . many University personnel were used to the
very decentralized, self-centered nature of University life and had a
difficult time orienting themselves to the task nature of the IMIS
project. . . . Another problem was the conflict between doing and
evaluation, i.e., if the University was to serve in an evaluation role,
also having an involvement in project development would create a
conflict of interest. This difficulty was resolved by removing the
University from operational concerns. The University seemed unable
to translate its many useful and worthwhile ideas into a coherent
program of activities.[14]

Marked as it was by high ambition, innocence of the probable complexities, a superfluity of actors, and rapid turnover of
key participants, USAC well exemplified many federal programs of the 1960s. But it also displayed three difficulties
which bore more directly on the problems of the university as
a provider and the city as a receiver of assistance. The first was
that, in Edwards's plaintive words, "It was never clear what the
university could do." The universities' uncertain role was almost certainly due in part to the fact that the design and the
funding of the projects had been undertaken by a third party.
Had city agencies contracted directly for assistance and paid
with their own funds, such systematic ambiguity would not
have been likely. The second important failing was the lack of
relevant competence in the participating urban governments.
Virtually none of the participating city agencies possessed the
technical capacity either to understand the difficulty of the
enterprise or to insure that the machinery and procedures
being offered by the data-processing firms would meet real
needs. As a 1976 National Academy of Sciences report on
USAC observed, "The successful use of technical consultation
requires that local governments contract for clearly defined
objectives and have the internal technical capability to manage

and monitor the fulfillment of the contract."[15] Throughout the USAC program, that capability was absent.*

A third deficiency was lack of concern. Each of the participating city agencies would have been pleased to acquire advanced data-processing capabilities; the new systems promised public relations as well as substantive benefits. But in no city were they critically important. They were not central to the plans of department heads or mayors and had not originally been sought by city officials. Federal agencies had provided the initial impulse, and the systems firms had amplified it. In almost every case the systems firms had written the city's proposal. This was not "demand-pull" innovation, therefore, but "supply-push." So city agencies rarely had reason to use to the full even the limited capacity they possessed to insure that the new capabilities met their needs. The results were systems designed to perform the tasks most interesting to the designers rather than those most helpful to the users.

THE URBAN TECHNOLOGY SYSTEM

A third federally-sponsored effort to stimulate urban innovation involved universities less directly but provides some suggestive evidence nonetheless.

The Urban Technology System (UTS) is a nationwide attempt to increase technological innovation in urban government by placing a Technology Agent (TA)—in effect, a broker —in the immediate office of the chief administrative officer of each of thirty-one cities and counties. The participating jurisdictions span the country, having been semirandomly selected from all cities and counties with populations between 50,000

---

*The consequences of the unfamiliarity of city officials with enterprises of this kind were not limited to the design of the data systems. For example, HUD's payments of USAC funds were made in accordance with complex cost-reimbursement contracts, arrangements unknown to most local officials. In Wichita Falls, this led to good faith city expenditures of some $50,000 which HUD refused to cover—and thus to protracted conflict.[16]

and 500,000. The program began in 1974, funded by the National Science Foundation. It is operated by Public Technology Incorporated (PTI), a private, nonprofit entity organized by the International City Management Association and linked, during its first years, to all major public interest groups concerned with local government. PTI's main business is to attempt to stimulate broader use of new technology in such standard municipal services as fire fighting, street repair, and trash collection; we discuss its means for doing this in chapter 4.

At its inception the program worked this way. The TAs, all engineers selected and trained with some care, circulated informally through city agencies, attempting to identify problems that the application of new technology might solve or ameliorate. Problems discovered were referred to one of fifteen* back-up centers (commercial or not-for-profit research organizations, or universities having appropriate interest and technical capability) for solution. If no solution could be worked out within ten man-days of effort, a fuller statement of the problem was circulated among the other TAs. If interest in their agencies was sufficiently strong, further work was authorized. Planned variations in the size and financial characteristics of the jurisdictions chosen and in the type and proximity of the back-up centers were designed to help identify the circumstances most conducive to technological change in local government.

Most interesting from our perspective are three observations, two about brokers of innovation, one concerning universities. By universal agreement, the variable most important to the successful operation of the program has been the TA —the mediator between municipality and technology. Espe-

---

*Cuts in the level of NSF funding during recent years have reduced the number of back-up centers from fifteen to five and somewhat diminished their role.

cially in the first years of UTS, what proved essential was that the TA win the trust of local officials. This typically required a nonthreatening personality; a willingness to identify problems first and only then to search for a useful technical solution (rather than starting from a favorite technology and searching for situations in which to apply it); and a concern to prove genuinely useful, whether that meant designing complex new computer applications or undertaking far more homely tasks, such as establishing efficient document reproduction practices.

More recent years of the program, however, suggest that it may be hard for TAs to combine sensitivity to the politics and the bureaucratics of local government with a continuing concern for innovation. Partly because of the reduction of NSF funding (cities now pay 90 percent of each TA's salary plus fringes as opposed to 10 percent minus fringes at the start of the program), UTS has lost to the participating cities much of its former control over who is appointed a TA and what he does. TAs are now more likely to be drawn from backgrounds in public administration than from technical fields and are more likely to regard themselves as part of the municipal administration. One close observer believes that although some TAs have thereby become more influential inducers of change, a larger number now fit too comfortably into local bureaucracies to push very hard for innovation. The observation is a useful reminder that agents of change must be accepted by local officials without seeking that acceptance above all. It is a difficult role.

The final observation concerns universities. Of the fifteen original back-up sites, five were private, for-profit research or engineering firms. Four were nonprofit institutes or federal laboratories. Five were universities: Texas A & M, North Carolina State, University of California at Berkeley, University of

Oklahoma, and Worcester Polytechnic. One was the Urban Observatory of Nashville, Tennessee, which drew on six local universities. At present, two universities, Texas A & M and U.C. Berkeley, remain in the program. UTS therefore permits some guarded inferences about the relative effectiveness of universities as against quite different institutions as sources of usable technical advice to urban governments.

James Murcer, PTI's first director of the UTS Project, believes that during his directorship the pattern was clear. Of the three types of back-up centers, "The non-profits were the best; the universities were worst." But Murcer also notes that variability within the categories of back-up sites may have been as great as the differences among them. Where participating universities chose as a point of contact for the TA someone actively committed to making the university helpful, university performance was not bad—especially in view of the funding arrangements: most universities absorbed 75 percent of the costs of back-up service and were reimbursed only for 25 percent. Higher proportions were reimbursed to all other centers.[17]

Murcer's comments are based on his impressions during the early history of the program. More systematic and more recent evidence tends partially to confirm and partially to modify his conclusions. A detailed internal assessment of the performance of the back-up centers conducted by PTI in the summer of 1976 assigned highest mean scores to the not-for-profits and lowest to the universities. The highest-rated university, moreover, scored below the highest-scoring back-up center in each of the other two categories, and the lowest-rated university scored below the lowest-rated center in each other category. Together with less quantitative evidence, the survey led PTI's UTS director to conclude that the relations between back-up sites and the TAs were crucial (an energetic

and well-motivated leadership being able to make any back-
up center useful), and that university representatives based in
an interdisciplinary center, rather than a classical academic
department, or having the support of high administrative officials tend to induce good university performance. And
though the performance of universities as a class lagged behind that of other back-up centers—most of them institutions to which short-term consulting was a far more familiar
enterprise—the performance of some improved considerably
over time. The work of Texas A & M, for example, is uniformly praised.[18]

Local Efforts

In virtually all American universities during the 1960s and early
1970s some effort took place to provide factual or analytic
assistance to a local government. In scale, subject, seriousness,
duration, and outcome, those efforts were enormously diverse.
Some enjoyed the support of deans and provosts, others proceeded despite their opposition. Some were based in interdisciplinary urban or public policy centers designed expressly to
produce such assistance; others in traditional departments or
in extension divisions. Some enjoyed substantial funding from
state or federal agencies, or from foundations (almost none
from cities); others scrounged funds, bootlegged professional
time, and impressed student volunteers. Some were grandiose
in conception; others modest. Some drew on genuine and
well-tested fields of expertise, others on "sciences" whose first
principles remain to be discovered. No comprehensive canvas
of that experience is possible here. But the histories of several
such ventures may be sketched; taken together, they appear to
be broadly representative.

"THE PROFESSORS OF THE CITY"

In 1962, with Ford Foundation funding, the University of Oklahoma began a program in "Urban Science." "The object of the 'Urban Science' program was to erect a platform for a comprehensive, holistic approach to urban problems and to elevate the study and remedy of urban problems to a science. An intervening 'urban scientist' was placed in each extension office to work toward developing closer university-community relationships."[19] By the university's own standards, the program had only a very limited success. The urban scientists and their graduate students were pressed to perform odd jobs and data gathering, but the city departments for which they worked continued to regard their own responsibilities as controlling and quite independent of any "holistic" approach. The Ford grant expired in 1964.

In the following year, however, The Higher Education Act of 1965 was passed. Title I of the act authorized grants to strengthen universities' community service programs. The University of Oklahoma then organized a consortium which included Tulsa University, the predominantly black Langston University, Oklahoma State, and the City of Tulsa. The consortium applied for and received a Title I grant of $80,000, supplemented by $20,000 from the City of Tulsa. Under the general supervision of an advisory council composed of one senior administrative official from each of the universities and an equal number of civic leaders (none of them city officials) the project was headed by a full-time project director with a small staff of his own. It employed some five or six (the number fluctuating over the life of the project) "Professors of the City." The professors were to provide research and planning expertise to various community agencies, with the staff supplying back-up support and aiding in implementation.

The activities the professors actually undertook varied extraordinarily. Largest in scale was their effort to help the city meet the elaborate planning and citizen participation requirements of its model city application. The application was successful, and the professors' leadership in preparing it was widely acknowledged. But the work had precipitated prolonged conflict among various community groups and between community groups and city agencies. The professors had clearly taken sides in those disputes, and by the end of the model cities application process, they were viewed by the city government "as agents of change, rather than resources for assistance."[20]

That image was made all the more vivid by an account of Tulsa's youth culture published by one of the professors. From 200 unstructured interviews, he produced *Talking with Tulsa Teens,* a wholly uncensorious report on teenage drinking, drug-use, shoplifting, exasperation with adult values, and alienation from public institutions. The report was widely read and heatedly discussed. In both its findings and tone it was regarded by the city's establishment as scandalous.

Some of the work of the project was more directly useful to Tulsa's government. The professors, for example, conducted management seminars for city executives and produced various reports for Tulsa's health and welfare agencies. But more characteristic were efforts to create a Tulsa Ecumenical Center devoted to "the making of one spirit through the coordination of diverse interests in the well being of the people of greater Tulsa," and a psyche of the city project which, in ten two-hour sessions, sought to have its twenty participants

confront specific problems as they actually occur in Tulsa and evaluate those problems in the holistic thinking of Leading Societalists, Ethologists, Auxologists and Mystigogues, thereby becoming aware of (1) the complexity of the problems, (2) the effect of their own predispositions on interpreting and solving the problems, and (3) the need for a rational context in which to deal with the problem.[21]

The "Professors of the City" program terminated in 1970. Federal funding had run out and the expected support of Tulsa's business community had proven impossible to elicit. Its principal monuments were the model city planning documents, the raised consciousnesses of some, and the outraged expectations of others.

THE CINCINNATI STORIES

Cincinnati offers at least two stories of interest. The first is discouraging.

In 1971, Cincinnati seemed to present a virtually ideal environment for effective university assistance to the city's government. For a city of its size, Cincinnati supported a rich cultural life. It honored intellectual endeavor and took pride in a history of efficient, forward-looking and nonpartisan municipal government. The University of Cincinnati, unlike virtually all other universities bearing the names of cities, was neither private nor part of the state system of higher education.* It received some state assistance but was basically city supported. Warren Bennis, the university's new president, was a prominent analyst of social change and organizational innovation, an activist by temperament, and (as suggested in the previous chapter) publicly dedicated to the highest conceptions of a university's responsibility to its host city.

Cincinnati's city manager, moreover, was E. Robert Turner, a highly regarded professional who, in previous city management posts, had worked with the universities of Oregon, Colorado, Southern California, and Michigan. Bennis and

---

*In 1971, the City University of New York was the only other exception.

Turner had known each other previously, and each respected the other.

Working cooperatively, Turner and Bennis secured a commitment of federal support for a consortium of university and city officials. They inaugurated the consortium in 1972 by personally leading a two-day "retreat" at which academics and city officials traded views of the city's problems and discussed ways the university might address them. A coordinating body was established. An Office of Metropolitan Affairs, headed by a vice-president, was set up to focus and direct the effort within the university. The consortium then sponsored a work-study program which placed UC students of city planning, engineering, and public administration in city offices; it commissioned a UC professor to design a method of projecting city income tax revenues; and it expended great effort on the development, by a dozen faculty members, of a system for bringing citizens' views to bear on the process of setting objectives for city agencies.

The work-study program remains usefully in existence, and the revenue projection system has proved modestly helpful. But the citizen participation structure is largely abandoned, the consortium itself fell quickly into disuse (leaving federal funds unspent), and the experience is universally regarded as a failure. "A disaster," is Turner's own characterization.

The explanations offered by participants and observers are varied but not inconsistent. On the university side, incentives were missing. "The money was there, but not the credit. It didn't do you any good with your department to work for a city agency, despite Bennis's interest," remarked one participant. A city official argued that "the professors who wanted to help were those who didn't already have clients. And they had only 'ideas,' mostly critical ones. They sounded like antagonists, not helpers." And some city officials believed that, while seeking federal funds for its own work with Cincinnati, the university tried to block federal support for work with the city proposed by Miami University of Ohio. Whether accurate or not, the belief reflects the sense of many officials that the university saw the city's needs principally as an opportunity for itself.

Shortcomings on the city side may have been more important. Turner's style of management put great stress on centralized oversight by strong staff offices reporting to him and less on innovation stimulated by the operating departments themselves. Accordingly, the city's representatives on the consortium were the city solicitor, the personnel director, and an assistant to the city manager. As an aide to Turner's successor remarked, Turner and Bennis both "wanted to act as funnels, not as catalysts." The funnels proved too narrow.

But it does not follow that the University of Cincinnati provided the city no help. Quite independently of the consortium, a number of individual professors and graduate students produced useful advice and assistance for city agencies. Successful in-service training programs were arranged for employees of the city's planning and budget offices. The municipal garage developed more efficient maintenance schedules with help from the engineering faculty, and the fire department and water and sewer agencies also used faculty engineers as consultants. Members of the design and architecture faculty routinely advised the Department of Development, the Cincinnati Health Department drew UC medical faculty into various advisory bodies, and the board of education depended heavily on education and educational administration faculty for help in curriculum development and other functions. The city management services office drew routinely on the skills of faculty members in the business school and in the economics and engineering departments. Such less visible, less formal, lower-level, ad hoc relations between city and university produced readily usable results, and they have endured.

A survey of these relationships was undertaken in late 1976 and, in the view of the city official who conducted it, its lessons are clear. First, funding was not a problem. "Where someone in a department has a real need, and he can find a professor he thinks can do him some good, finding the money is not that hard."* Second, what distinguished the agencies drawing most heavily on academic support was not any particular function or type of responsibility but simply the internal motivation to improve or innovate. Thirdly, the student cooperative program had helped considerably to keep current the acquaintanceships of professors and city officials. (This was true even for those city agencies, like the Planning Commission, whose professional staffs were graduates of UC; their working ties to the school showed a very short half-life after receipt of a final degree.) Finally, the survey showed that a personal relationship between supplier and consumer of advice is nearly essential. Formal contacts at high levels between city and university were sometimes helpful, but never necessary and never sufficient. "You've got to build bridges lower down."

Turner's assertion that the consortium had been a "disaster" was countered, during one discussion, by evidence of successful and numerous cooperative relationships at lower levels. "Yeah, but that didn't do me any good," was his response. The remark tends to confirm the "funnel versus catalyst" diagnosis. It also suggests that the questions of whose purposes are served by innovation—who gets political credit for it and who benefits from the bureaucratic leverage that accompanies control of research funds—are important ones.[22]

THE OAKLAND PROJECT

In 1969, James Webb, head of the National Aeronautics and Space Administration (NASA), was also president of the American Society for Public Administration. As a matter of

---

*HUD 701 money paid for some of it, Cincinnati general funds for some; the rest was simply volunteered.

personal conviction Webb believed that American cities could benefit greatly from the systematic application of technical advice. As a matter of NASA's future, with its space exploits ending and a tidal shift in national priorities becoming evident, Webb thought it useful to demonstrate "spin-off" benefits from both the technology and the management skills that had put Americans on the moon. At the same time Clark Kerr, chancellor of the University of California, and Wayne Thompson, city manager of Oakland, California, were interested in showing that universities could provide important technical and managerial assistance to cities. And Oakland clearly deserved attention: economically depressed and racially divided, it was a tinderbox. One result was a NASA grant of some $120,000 to the University of California at Berkeley for two years of "technology transfer" focused on Oakland.

Linkages with Oakland officials were undertaken by policy-oriented faculty from several departments, including mathematics, regional planning, and political science. Graduate students were placed as aides to Oakland's mayor and city manager; a useful catalogue of federal programs operating in Oakland was compiled (federal disbursements in Oakland, roughly $100 million annually, were twice Oakland's own budget); and students and faculty observed and worked with black community groups, offered the Oakland police proposals for reallocations of their budget, attempted work for the fire department and for the finance and city planning offices, and engaged in a detailed and critical study of the Oakland library system. The same experiences were used to develop teaching materials, dissertations, and other studies.

What Oakland itself received from this activity was little in one sense, rather more in another. The relationship with the Oakland police department failed; the department's chief interest was in new equipment, not policy analysis. Studies of new clothing, hoses, and communication equipment were performed for the fire department, but no important practices or policies of the department were affected by them. Neither the police nor fire departments were interested in mathematical models. The library system was little moved by the program's critical analysis, and a long delay in completing the study annoyed Oakland's city manager who had first proposed it. But some student papers prepared independently of the work requested by Oakland proved influential. A study proposing use of the city's pension funds to finance housing rehabilitation, for example, led indirectly to the adoption of that practice. But probably most helpful was the steady, informal, ad hoc assistance rendered to a number of Oakland's officials by the graduate students assigned to them.

The clearest case was Arnold Meltsner's work for Oakland's new city manager, Jerome Keithley. Though still a graduate student, Meltsner had worked at the RAND Corporation and served as a consultant to the systems analysis staff in the office of the secretary of defense. Direct and unpretentious in manner and determined to prove helpful, Meltsner served two principal functions. He became an analytically-oriented general-purpose assistant to the city manager and a mediator and broker between city and university. Keithley possessed no staff of his own, had access to no analytic resources, indeed "had no one to talk to." Since the manager was accustomed to arriving at his office early, Meltsner made it a practice to arrive early as well. "Then there was time to talk with him over coffee, and get a sense of what really mattered to him."[23] Acquisition of that sense of what mattered led Meltsner to troubleshooting and speech writing, but he also undertook an extended study of Oakland's sources of revenue, an analysis that clarified the city's financial position and produced several feasible proposals for marginally improving it.

Meltsner's roots in the university and closeness to decision making in Oakland also made him an effective broker. He identified problems whose analysis would interest municipal officials (library practices and budgets), specified for other academics the nature of the environment in which their work would be received, and spotted situations in which other graduate students might usefully be placed.

So a program whose initial ambitions were to transfer technology and apply sophisticated methods of management succeeded at neither but did provide administrators with one-man personal staffs and some well-targeted if methodologically straightforward studies. NASA had little useful hardware to transfer, the university had none, and Oakland was not ready for advanced management. But the city could use simpler forms of assistance, and a number of faculty members and graduate students, by departing from the usual model of methodologically rigorous, objective, and self-contained research, proved able to provide it.

SANITATION AND STONY BROOK

New York City's Department of Sanitation in 1970 was an unlikely client for university-based research. Its 11,000 workers looked to a tough, resourceful, and politically powerful union boss for leadership and tolerated little management from departmental superiors. They disposed of some 20,000 tons of garbage and refuse daily, absorbed a budget of some $200 million annually, and followed work patterns essentially unchanged for forty years. But the department was strained by the large annual increases in the waste the city generated—increases larger than could continuously be accommodated by enlarging the sanitation work force, and the Lindsay administration was then determined to press for efficiency gains throughout the city government, using external advisers and experts to help achieve them.

Meanwhile, early in 1970, a program for urban and policy

sciences had been established at the State University of New York at Stony Brook. The Stony Brook campus, some sixty miles east of Manhattan on Long Island, housed the one graduate center of the fast-growing State University of New York oriented toward the hard sciences. The principal purpose of the new program was to train policy analysts. It offered a two-year course in economics, statistics, mathematics, and engineering, leading to a master's degree. But the program had been established by new faculty deeply interested in performing useful research for local governments,* and it was well designed to serve that purpose. The program had obtained the authority, rare among its counterparts elsewhere, to hire, promote, and fire its own faculty. And the program enjoyed strong support from the university's president. A three-month internship with a government agency was part of the curriculum, and a two-year $500,000 grant from the National Science Foundation (NSF) was available to support full-time research associates. The program was thus equipped with motivation, money, and quantitative analytic skill; all it lacked were clients.

Late in 1970 Stony Brook faculty introduced themselves to officials of the Department of Sanitation and proposed to perform various analyses. The response was skeptical. The academics persisted, offering to address whatever problems the department thought important and to meet rigid time-deadlines in proposing solutions. As it happened, the department faced several problems that were technical as well as political and that the analytic competence of the Stony Brook researchers was well suited to address. One such question was whether changes in work schedules could increase productivity and prove attractive to sanitation workers at the same time. The city's own analysts, lodged both in the Budget Bureau and in

*Robert Nathan, the physicist who chaired the program, had left the Brookhaven Laboratories principally because of the Laboratory's unwillingness to allow policy-oriented work.

the Environmental Protection Agency (EPA) (the "Supcragency" of which the Department of Sanitation was now part), had noted an anomaly. Sanitation work schedules placed crews of identical size on duty Mondays through Saturdays, but the volume of refuse to be collected varied markedly by the days of the week. The pattern, moreover, was quite predictable: Monday loads were heavy, the mid-week was light. Under then-current practice, night and Sunday collections were used to balance out the workload. But the overtime costs were high, and work at off-hours was resented by some of the men and annoyed the public.

A number of favorable conditions were now conjoined. One was that, as a participant has remarked, "here was a problem that a linear programming model really could fit."[24] For another, the Stony Brook analysts wanted no fee; their NSF funding sufficed. A third was that pressure for some change in collection practices was already strong. Another was that the department's own staff understood what form a useful analysis would have to take. Indeed, a young graduate student in economics, serving as a summer intern to EPA's analytic and planning staff, was assigned to specify the problem. The resulting twenty-page paper described the alternative solutions already considered, noted the statutory and political constraints, and thus defined the analytic task with rare precision.

Effectively guided, Stony Brook professors, research associates, and graduate students systematically compared the probable costs and benefits of hiring additional men, regularizing overtime, or skewing the shifts to provide more men during regular hours on peak-load days. By a demonstrable margin of some $5 million annually, the last alternative proved preferable.

But lingering union opposition and the pressure of numerous working-level problems (rearranging car pools, scheduling special assignments, and accomodating the traditionally high rate of transfers of work places and time assignments) produced repeated postponements of proposed shifts to the new work schedules. At this point the academics, having resolved the conceptual problem, might well have considered their work done and gone on to another exercise fit for linear programming. Instead, Stony Brook assigned a young research associate (a recent graduate of the public policy program at Berkeley, as it happened) to one of the department's sixty-eight districts with instructions to continue working out the details until that district was prepared to test the new plan. The associate was well chosen; he exhibited patience, a friendly manner, respect for the sources of even trivial impediments, and a commitment to full implementation as the measure of his own success. Twelve months of negotiation, cajolery, the building of friendships, and paper-and-pencil tests of the plan were required before an operational trial could be run. But when run, the trial was successful. Two months later the new schedule was adopted citywide.[25]

Similar studies were thereafter performed on the queuing of collection trucks at the piers where refuse is dumped into barges; the scheduling and optimum number of barges; the value of mini-incinerators in scattered sites around the city; and the appropriate routing patterns for compactor trucks of differing capacities. Not all of these studies led to change in policy or in operations, but all looked closely at the real constraints on change. All but the last illuminated serious policy options and, in conjunction with the studies performed by EPA staff, each expanded the technical sophistication of the department's leadership and that of the union.

Interestingly, however, changes in the city's political leadership, coupled with shifts in the policy and research interests of Stony Brook faculty (many of whom are now concerned with energy issues at the national level), shortly thereafter ended the university's work with the Department of Sanitation.

MODEL BUILDING IN PITTSBURGH*

The Community Renewal Program (CRP) authorized by Congress in 1959 was founded on the belief that decisions concerning the renewal of urban housing and the rehabilitation of city neighborhoods should be made in the light of their probable effects on population shifts, transportation patterns, and local economic development. The statute therefore authorized the Housing and Home Finance Agency (HHFA) to make grants to local authorities to support the development of comprehensive local plans. The plans would identify local demographic and economic trends and attempt to set all relevant federal, state, and local renewal activities in their context. They would thus display for local decision makers the relationships among various forms of private and public action, clarify the relative virtues of alternative renewal projects, and provide a comprehensive framework for future decision making.

In February 1961, the city of Pittsburgh was awarded a $200,000 grant for the two-year development of such a CRP. The award had been made on essentially political grounds, however, and the city government then possessed neither the talent nor the incentive to utilize the money. For a year no progress was made. By early 1962, however, under pressure from the city's business leadership, the mayor's office had hired a new planning director, Calvin Hamilton. Chosen after a nationwide search, Hamilton was known for energy, innovation, and entrepreneurship, but not for technical analytical skills. He procured an additional grant from HHFA, bringing the funds available from all sources for the CRP to roughly $1.5 million. The city was to provide one-third of this sum, but only through "in-kind" services.

*This account relies heavily on Garry D. Brewer's penetrating study, *Politicians, Bureaucrats, and the Consultant*, (Basic Books: New York, 1973).

Pittsburgh's proposal, like the CRP program generally, had been conceptually ambitious. How could these various factors —policy variables, public and private investment decisions, transport, demographic and employment trends—be related? The first problem was simply to describe the factors correctly. Data were incomplete, unreliable, and inconsistent in form. Hamilton responded by hiring a new director of data processing, a graduate student at the University of Pittsburgh experienced in data handling and the building of models. The next problem was relating the variables. Having been appointed an adjunct professor at Pittsburgh, Hamilton consulted his academic colleagues. They proposed a series of linked mathematical models capable of simulating the probable consequences of alternative policy choices. Hamilton had little experience with modeling, but knew that his planning department could not develop such models without substantial assistance. He entered into a $215,000 contract with the Center for Regional Economic Studies (CRES) of the University of Pittsburgh, under which CRES was broadly required to "supplement, assist, help guide the work of the department, and evaluate the results of the program."[26]

CRES was less than six months old. It had been established to perform economic analyses of the Pittsburgh region (which a Ford Foundation grant supported) and was staffed by economists and social scientists. It had handled no contract of this size and lacked the specialized competence in computers which the CRP would require. CRES therefore subcontracted with the California-based CONSAD Research Corporation for "computer support." CONSAD had extensive computer and simulation experience but had performed no research on urban issues and had no experience with local government clients.

Data problems immediately proved formidable. The mayor refused to grant Hamilton permission to require other city departments to produce what he needed, and the departments, unhappy at the work involved and probably wary of the potential for embarrassment as important data proved inconsistent or absent, declined to supply it voluntarily. Estimates and projections were therefore made on slim and impressionistic evidence or on none. The result was that the first-stage submodel of the CRP, intended to calculate future industrial employment levels in the Pittsburgh region, yielded information of doubtful validity for the other submodels to process. The next submodel, produced, like the first, by CONSAD, was intended to relate the industrial employment patterns generated by the first submodel to individual census tracts. But it was based on assumed site-selection criteria that had no observable relation to those actually used in industry. Even on optimistic assumptions about the quality of the data it used, its predictive value was therefore wholly speculative. The final component was a submodel intended to specify the extent and location of retail employment and of the city's residential population implied by the outputs of the prior submodels. This last component, designed by CRES, was based on a pathbreaking model previously developed as a research device, not a predictor, that had been clearly labeled by its designer as "unusable at this point for any serious practical purpose."[27] And it required data which the prior submodels could not supply.

The conceptual and technical limitations of the CRP models were compounded, as it happened, by other shortcomings —in the relations of Hamilton, CONSAD and CRES to each other and to the city government for which they were nominally working.

Confident, expansive, and oriented toward the national urban planning community, Hamilton publicized the project across the country in speeches and articles. But he failed to find terms on which his staff could work with the city's Housing or

Redevelopment Authorities or with the county Redevelopment Agency—the bodies which, together with the mayor and city council, would determine whether the CRP was to have any operational effect. Moreover, his planning staff contained no one technically competent to contribute to or even to assess what CONSAD and CRES were doing. Finally, the staff was far more comfortable dealing with the supportive federal agencies than with their Pittsburgh colleagues. "City Hall was always quite skeptical. But we always one-upped them because we were always able to establish real rapport and gain respect of people in Washington. We didn't need the Mayor's Office."[28] It was a poor strategy and a mistaken estimate.

Isolated from the city's decision makers, utilizing data and modeling techniques unlikely to prove reliable, but committed to proceeding, CONSAD focused on the technical accomplishments of its model building and reinforced Hamilton's claims of success in the planning community and in Washington. Brewer quotes one participant's observations:

> You know, the thing is not working, but I don't think the profession as a whole is aware of this, let alone the outside world. The articles which appear in the *AIP Journal (Journal of the American Institute of Planners),* for example, suggest that everything is coming up roses. The *Journal* has had whole issues devoted to models . . . (CONSAD's President) had an article (in one); it was very glowing and there was no hint of the fact that we've got something here that hasn't produced very much.[29]

CRES's performance appears to have combined all the faults of which university-based policy research is commonly accused. The associate director who figured prominently in CRES's acceptance of the CRP contract left the university in mid-1963, just as the work began. His replacement, new to the project, found that the CRES staff possessed neither the motivation nor the skill to perform its own work while supervising its subcontractor; he found also that the budget precluded staff increases. CRES members were also teaching and, as one of them estimated, "I spent at least 85 to 90 percent of my time preparing courses and working on them, and the remaining time, as I found it, went into research."[30] Matters were made more difficult by the low regard the academics held for the city officials they had agreed to assist and for the "irrational" political considerations that carried such weight with those officials. (Brewer quotes one academic as announcing that cities "are run by low-level bums.")

Bums or not, city officials had hold of an important truth: the university had sought a job, been given a job, and was failing to do the job. One Pittsburgh politician observed, "They have a lot of people out there who overload themselves with consulting and who do a half-assed job, who do as little as they can get away with."[31] CRES's new project leader adopted the tactic, understandable under the circumstances, of a quick kick.

> I made this strategic decision to shift the responsibility to CON-SAD. . . . The subcontract to them got increased (and so on). . . . I successfully created a situation where the City Planning Department viewed (CONSAD and CRES) as jointly responsible. It did not view me as responsible for them, which was a great mercy. It was one of my more skillful administrative achievements. I thought there was a bomb there. I thought you really couldn't deliver for the kind of money and time what was promised. I really didn't believe it was possible; and CONSAD kept believing it was possible.[32]

It wasn't possible, and when that became clear, the predictable followed. Hamilton, lacking any political base, was fired. His successor was the mayor's urban renewal coordinator, a former newsman and publicist. The Planning Department's staff was purged of everyone who had worked on the CRP. When CONSAD asked the new director for a six-month extension of the contract to allow receipt of additional federal funding already authorized by HHFA, the request was refused.

The project was over. The city government had received nothing it could use, its resistance to comprehensive planning had been reinforced, and its instincts as to the utility of university-based consulting had been confirmed.

CHAPTER 3

Of All Men Least Fitted

Scholars are of all men those least fitted for politics and its ways. The reason for this is that they
are accustomed to intellectual speculation, the
search for concepts and their abstraction from
sense-data . . . they do not, in general, seek to
make their thoughts conform to external reality,
but rather deduce what ought to exist outside
from what goes on in their minds.

Now those who engage in politics must pay
great attention to what goes on outside, and to all
the circumstances that accompany and succeed
an event. Hence men of learning, who are accustomed to generalizations and the extensive use of
analogy, tend, when dealing with political affairs,
to impose their own frame of concepts and deduc-
tions on things, thus falling into error.

IBN KHALDUN
The Muqaddimah *

Long and varied as it is, the record of university-based efforts
to provide usable advice to American city governments may
well support sharply differing assessments. But it is striking
that, self-serving accounts aside, almost all commentary agrees
with the impression produced by the histories we have just

---

*Less illuminating but more pungent is Bismarck's remark: "It makes no difference
what sort of person becomes Chancellor provided he isn't a professor."

reviewed; it pronounces this record a failure. Casual conversation among policy-oriented academics is spiked with horror
stories, snidely or ruefully delivered. The attitudes most common among urban officials range from the bitter to the derisive,
echoing the statements quoted above in Pittsburgh's case or
the assessment by Cleveland's planning director of three university-based policy studies in that city: "Though each of these
studies was directed at a different issue and each encountered
different problems, they have one thing in common: none of
them had any visible effect on public policy."[1]

A 1970 survey of attitudes among Massachusetts environmental officials found the officials interested in developing
effective working relations with universities but, unsurpris-
ingly, fearful that academics would disdain their policy concerns and "rework problems into something more of academic
significance than of practical value."[2] More comprehensive
evidence was provided by a survey undertaken in the same year
by the International City Management Association. Question-
naires sent to the chief administrative officers of each of the
859 U.S. cities with populations over 25,000 were designed to
identify the sources of advice those officials used on scientific
and technical issues and to determine the administrators' rat-
ings of relative usefulness of those sources. Two hundred
ninety five officials responded. Of those who reported drawing
scientific and technical advice from city personnel, 68 percent
rated that source "Very Useful." Of those who utilized private
consulting firms, 72 percent counted them "Very Useful." Of
the 164 administrators who reported that they sought such
advice from universities or colleges, only 39 percent rated that
source as "Very Useful."[3] Those results should be treated
gingerly; they refer to only one type of advice, received at only
one level of government. And since the respondents were
themselves responsible for the relationships they were rating,
the assessments are probably more favorable than other observ-

ers might have made. The relative scores, nonetheless, are striking.

Typical of the few well-informed comments by outsiders was this 1974 assessment of William C. Pendleton of the Ford Foundation:

> I would guess that although there have been several mutually satisfying tie-ins between academics and officeholders, the failures outnumber the successes by at least ten to one. It remains questionable whether any progress has been made toward developing productive working relations between university people and urban leaders.[4]

FAILURE EXPLAINED

The reasons given for failure, interestingly, are highly consistent. Most are based on the observation that the cultures of universities and of local government are vastly different.* That view, of course, is not novel, nor is its application confined to local policy making. As Max Millikan has observed about applied research generally:

> The scientist is apt to have a strong conviction that applied research cannot be 'fundamental,' that there is something inherently contradictory in the advance of knowledge and the service of practical ends. . . . The researcher may face a growing conviction either that the operator has asked the wrong questions, that the questions are too vaguely or too narrowly formulated, or that as formulated they are incapable of being clearly answered.[5]

Martin Rein and Sheldon White have pointed out that where applied work relates to public policy, the contradictions deepen:

> The painfulness of the alliance (between analysts and policy-makers) arises out of the fundamental incompatibility of the games of

---

*"Yes," agreed one academic informant, "the politics of local government is not nearly so vicious."

science and the games of politics. The games of science seek to establish patterns of experience that all may share. They are value-neutral in the sense that they are deliberately designed to filter out the values of the participants so as to arrive at the "unbiased truth." Best play in such games leads to assertions of findings that must be accepted by individuals whether they find them palatable or unpalatable. The proper posture for a gamesman of science must be one of restraint, dispassion, conservatism, the willingness to suspend belief pending more evidence. Now the games of politics are quite different. They are designed to find one purpose or course of action acceptable to individuals who enter espousing diverse purposes, values, and courses of action. They are value-expressive, and facts enter in only as subordinated to and sustaining values, only as they contribute to the delineation of an issue. Best play in such games leads towards the maximum possible satisfaction of one's purposes in the group action. The proper posture for a gamesman of politics must be one of boldness, persistence, opportunism, the ability to mobilize and sustain belief and commitment.

It is extremely difficult for an individual to hold credibility in these two very different kinds of games. Generally, the scientific gamesman who is too action-oriented loses credibility and, in pretty much the same way, the political gamesman who is too theory-oriented loses credibility. But the basic problem is not one of the ability or inability but of an incompatibility of the two games. One trades in facts and the other in values.[6]

Even where scholars have failed to notice the incompatibility, or are prepared to overlook it or to adopt the values of politics, other impediments remain. Most faculty members are trained and accustomed to work alone or, at most, in small groups of scholars in their own discipline. But the analysis of a significant policy problem almost always requires several perspectives and a number of disciplines. An academic working alone, or with only familiar colleagues, will therefore tend to respond merely to a piece of a problem, and perhaps only a quite small piece. As many have pointed out, moreover, most faculty members are rewarded only as scholars and teachers, especially the former. The approval they seek is that of their peers, and that depends on the quality and number of their scholarly publications; the informal, nondisciplinary, and often verbal communications most useful to a governmental client do not qualify. Indeed, while failing to win academic credit, such actions may produce public criticism. "Who wants to sit with his family watching the evening news on T.V. as some city council member attacks his findings or questions his motives?" asked one academic informant.[7]

Finally, the roles and powers of university administrators are quite unlike executives in business or government. Many local officials tend to assume that a dean, provost, or president of a university speaks for his institution as a corporate executive or bureau director speaks for his. But academics know that "universities may have presidents, but presidents don't have universities." Academic administrators rarely deploy significant resources; the usual terms of academic employment mean that faculty members must be enticed into new commitments, and on terms satisfactory to them.

In a thoughtful talk subsequent to the address previously quoted,[8] William Pendleton specified a number of additional obstacles. The first echoes Ibn Khaldun:

. . . university scholars seek answers that are true and general; city officials, in contrast, need answers that are specific and will work. The academic researcher, particularly in the social sciences, gathers data so that he can support generalizations about large numbers of people, cities, employers, and so forth. Such findings only accidentally provide useful guidance to the individual person, city, or employer. Because the research is pursued for its contribution to knowledge, it is often clearly inappropriate as a guide to action. But the city decision-maker needs answers to *his* problems, advice that fits the particular characteristics of *his* city.

A second problem, Pendleton added, is that

. . . scholars and politicians frequently speak different languages.
Most academic disciplines have developed their own technical jargon
for making communication among members of the discipline faster
and more precise. But such jargon is totally inappropriate in negotiat-
ing with the police chief or in advising the director of public works,
and is certainly not to be used to communicate the findings of a
research project that has been paid for with city funds.

Another difficulty Pendleton noted

. . . grows directly out of the more relaxed lifestyle of the academic.
Scholars and politicians live on different time schedules. The planning horizon on the campus tends to be the semester or the academic
year; at City Hall the relevant time periods are usually days or weeks.
Consequently, academics are often not available when needed, and
their research results often appear well after the problem has disappeared. It is slight comfort to a mayor to be told by the scholar that
he'll be back with an answer in two years, particularly when the next
election is eighteen months away.

Finally, Pendleton pointed out that

Professors tend to know very little about how city government is
organized—where responsibility for different functions lies, and who
fills key jobs. A similar unfamiliarity with universities pervades the
city bureaucracy. People in the two institutions don't know each
other, don't know each other's interests and capabilities, or the ways
in which they might work together, and no mechanism exists for
getting such information quickly.

At least three other sources of tension are worth specifying.
In an important empirical study of the use of social science in
federal policy decisions, Nathan Caplan and coauthors suggest
that most academics concern themselves only with what they
term the "internal logic" of an issue—a constrained and often
technical view of the nature of the problem. Policy makers,

thcy point out, tend to weigh far more heavily the "external logic"—the problem's political and bureaucratic ramifications.[9] "There is an observer's truth and a practitioner's truth," in Warren Bennis's phrase.

And even where the academic's angle of vision is as wide as the practitioner's, his training is likely to incline him to seek an original conclusion, a solution not previously proposed. It is a common complaint against bureaucrats that they resist anything "not invented here." But scholars may be worse in this respect; the academic culture values originality and priority of finding even more highly. The result is that while the policy maker wants a solution that will work (and the reliable, in general, has previously been tried), and while his subordinates will warm most willingly to a proposal whose basic lines are attributed to them, the scholar, taking pains to distinguish his work from the previously understood, typically proposes untested novelty.[10] Public discourse of the 1960s treated "innovation" as synonymous with "improvement"; for that reason a mayor might be intrigued by novelty. But the subordinates required to make it work, and to take the blame if it did not, were generally more skeptical. It is a familiar truth in local government that if you do the job the old way and something goes wrong, that's an act of God; but if you do it a new way and something goes wrong, it's your neck.

A final source of tension may be the most fundamental. Transforming a good proposal into an accomplished and accepted change in policy or operations is hard, long, and risky work. Adapting and testing the proposals of academics, persuading the skeptical, reassuring the threatened, obtaining the funds, procuring the equipment, attending to the details of implementation—these are the hard jobs. And at many points in the course of doing them the expertise of the proposer may be useful to call upon. But the scholar responsible for the proposal may be on sabbatical, overcommitted to teaching, or "into" something else. In any event, he is likely to regard *his* work as done. And the graduate students who may have actually performed the study and designed the proposal are even more ephemeral: they quit school, change fields, disappear during summers, become distracted by personal problems (or even by schoolwork), and they graduate.

These apparent incompatibilities between the cultures of the academy and of local government conceal a great deal. As we will argue later, they "explain" a result that, disconcertingly, occurs even in their absence. They also gloss over the very substantial differences *within* the two cultures. By and large, professors of engineering feel differently about an unimplementable "solution" from professors of sociology. Indeed, the attitudes toward applied research of teachers of engineering are probably closer to those of the engineers in municipal water departments than to those in many other academic de-

TABLE 3-1

	The Two Cultures	
Attributes	Academic	Governmental
1. Ultimate object	Respect of academic peers	Approval of electorate
2. Time horizon	Long	Short
3. Focus	Internal logic of the problem	External logic of the setting
4. Mode of thought	Inductive, generic	Deductive, particular
5. Mode of work	Solo	Collaborative
6. Most valued outcome	Original insight	Reliable solution
7. Mode of expression	Abstruse, qualified	Simple, absolute
8. Preferred form of conclusion	Multiple possibilities, depending on objective; uncertainties emphasized	One "best" solution, objectives unspecified, uncertainties submerged
9. Concern for feasibility	Small	Great
10. Stability of interest	Low	High

partments. Similarly, the values of city officials at high political levels differ greatly from those of their operating subordinates immersed in the technical and bureaucratic problems involved in collecting trash, fighting fires, or processing criminal complaints. There are several cultures, and numerous subcultures, in both communities. Nonetheless, the "two cultures" perception embodies some relevant crude truths; it is therefore useful to summarize.

THEREFORE, WHAT?

From this general agreement on the prevalence of failure, and on its deep and numerous causes, arise two sets of conclusions. They are strikingly different.

One is "back to scholarship." The argument here takes two forms, the first of which is obvious from the preceding discussion. It has been succinctly put by Provost Dixon Long of Case Western Reserve:

The people who are good at local politics spend eighteen hours a day at it, learning it, playing it. The people who are first-rate academically are just as single-minded. They spend eighteen waking hours deeply immersed in their academic specialty. What reason is there to think, then, that either one can successfully play the role of the other?[11]

The academic, then, is inherently unsuitable to the work. Much as he may wish to help (or want the money or welcome the distraction), he is out of his element, beyond his expertise. The second form of the argument is that the seeking of "relevance" not only fails to serve the city but perverts the university. It distracts and diverts. It dissipates the comparative advantage and ignores the responsibility of the scholar—namely, to study and to teach. Attempting what he does poorly, the scholar will also fail at what only he can do well.

The counterconclusion is that providing useful assistance to

public officials is even more important than it is difficult, and
that the obligations of universities include service as well as
scholarship. Interestingly, those who take this position tend
not to contest the arguments about the differing cultures of
scholarship and politics but rather to ignore them. They focus
instead on three less intractable reasons for poor prior performance: "improper organization" of the universities, inadequate incentives for scholars interested in applied work, and
insufficient funding.[12]

Notions of what is wrong with the organization of universities for public service vary widely; so, consequently, do the
proposed reforms. Earl Ferguson at Oklahoma State University, for example, has argued that to facilitate and manage
relations between campus and prospective client, special university offices need to be established. These would marshal
relevant expertise within the university and provide logistical
support and "follow-up activities."[13] President Ratchford of
the University of Missouri has stressed that while administrative officers must encourage and oversee the public service
function, the units principally responsible must be the academic departments, each department supporting one or many
faculty members whose main function is public service and
whose clients are local governments.[14] More common are assertions that what is needed are interdisciplinary units especially oriented toward applied work (but engaged also, it is
usually added, in training and research functions). A typical
statement is that urban universities must organize "permanent
trans-disciplinary urban affairs units to engage in pre-career,
and continuing education of local government personnel, as
well as to carry on applied research and service activities that
have special value to local government. Many such units do
exist but very few of them have the scale and unity of purpose
which is needed."[15]

The problem of incentives is treated with greater consistency. Robert Nathans, director of the Stony Brook program previously described, speaks for many in asserting that

> . . . faculty who wish to participate in this kind of activity must be treated as equals—which means the same potential for receiving promotion and tenure. Few faculty members receive the respect of their peers if they lack these prerogatives. This issue of faculty acceptance or academic respectability is a powerful operating influence in all universities. The long-term viability of university programs of the type I have been describing depends critically on receiving these acknowledgements.[16]

In the talk previously cited, President Ratchford similarly noted that "The rewards system for the individuals who choose to devote their time to public service functions must offer the same salaries and job security available to those involved with more traditional university activities." The Cleveland State University "urban strategy" proposal is more explicit:

> At present, the fact is that applied research on local problems often works directly against the interest of the faculty member when he is up for promotion. Individual faculty members may continue to indulge themselves in this kind of work, but they may also consider themselves fools for doing so. . . . Faculty have listened to too many exhortations and too many statements about the goals of the university, only to find that the sole activity which is rewarded in the university is scholarly publication in certain types of recognized journals. Vigor and ingenuity in the development of applied problems must be clearly rewarded if a statement about the urban mission of the university is to have any credibility.[17]

The argument that additional funding is required for urban-related work is also made universally, differing only in shading according to whether professors are arguing to provosts and presidents, or provosts and presidents are addressing state legislatures, foundation executives, or agencies of the federal government. It stresses that the additional funding, whatever its scale, must be "hard"—dependable and continuous enough to support the salaries of tenured faculty. Less attractively, it argues (or assumes) that the funds should move directly from some third party—foundation, federal agency, or state legislature—to the university, without passing through the hands of any supposed beneficiary of the advice to be produced.*

REASONS FOR SKEPTICISM

How is one to choose between these opposing arguments? Both reflect understanding that the record of universities in providing usable advice to local governments is poor. Both point for explanation to undeniable characteristics of universities as currently organized, staffed, and funded. Yet they point in opposite directions.

A first temptation is to conclude that as explanations both are partly right, the truth residing somewhere in between. As to prescription, then, the choice might be one of values: scholarship versus service. But second thoughts quickly intrude. Some will follow the lines of Carl F. Stover's argument in

---

*A July, 1975 paper entitled "Academic Public Service Program for State and Local Governments" written for the National Science Foundation by Gene A. Bramlett, an assistant vice-president for services of the University of Georgia, displays vividly this reluctance to let consumers of university-based assistance intervene in the relationship between the schools and their funders. Bramlett would assign responsibility for determining that a state is eligible for a federally-funded academic public service program to the presidents of two or three "of the major public universities in each state initially selected." He notes that a reasonable alternative would be to invite governors to submit applications for state eligibility but concludes that although governors and local officials should receive announcements of the program, making them responsible for applications "could result in extreme variations in the outcome."

Bramlett proposes that for five years planning grants and institutional grants to universities total some $700,000 annually while grants to state and local governments "to develop linkage systems" would come to $50,000. The whole of this funding would come from NSF in the first year, with none coming from state governments. Those proportions would reverse themselves over a five-year period, after which the states would undertake full funding of the program. These funds, it should be understood, buy nothing for any state or local government. They simply improve the institutional capacity of universities to provide assistance when asked. Actual assistance would have to be paid for on a project basis by additional state, federal, foundation, or requesting jurisdiction funds.

"Commentary on Recommendations for an Academic Public Service," a perceptive assessment of proposals of the kind just described, prepared for the National Science Foundation in 1976. Stover argues, in effect, that even if the value question be resolved in favor of service, substantial questions both of comparative advantage and of consumer choice remain. As to the first, he points out that local governments can seek advice from many sources other than universities and that at least some of these—consulting organizations and "think tanks," for example—may provide it more effectively. As to the second, Stover argues that local governmental "consumers" of service might most appropriately be left to choose their "producers" for themselves. If "academic public service" is to be publicly supported, Stover asks, then why not "industrial public service," or "independent professionals public service?"

Those questions have weight, and we return to them at the conclusion of this study. Other objections spring to mind. One is that the estimate of failure in these university-city relationships is partly a result of expectations that, in retrospect, seem naive and overstated: against more reasonable standards many relationships of scholars and decision makers would be judged fruitful. Another is that patterns can be discerned in the relationships, and the patterns suggest the kinds of linkages that work and the circumstances under which they work best. To these points, too, we will return.

But a prior and larger proposition should first be set out and defended. It is that all of the conventional discussion of academic public service and of the provision of advice by universities to local government misses a large, indeed a dominating, truth. The truth is that neither changed incentives nor improved organization in the universities, nor assured funding, nor more discriminating use of those academic disciplines having most to offer local decision makers, nor more careful selection of the problems on which well-qualified academics are to work are likely to greatly improve the low success rate of such work. The reason is that the conventional discussion is profoundly misleading. Examining a set of largely unproductive relationships, it looks almost entirely to the characteristics of one party—the universities—to explain their failure. Correspondingly, its proposals for improvement seek changes in the universities. But a wider body of evidence strongly suggests that the binding constraint on the effective use by local government of external advice and expertise is not any shortage or defect in the supply of good ideas. It is the limited ability and weak incentives of local officials to seek, absorb, and attempt to apply such ideas in the face of the political, bureaucratic, and fiscal limitations that bind them. Improvement in the "supply" side of the relationship, in short, can be helpful and may be necessary, but it will rarely prove sufficient. More efficient urban services and more effective urban policies require either that the "consuming" side of the advice relationship gain a far greater capacity to use the advice available, or that the producing side radically expand its role and responsibilities.

We turn now to the evidence for that proposition.

CHAPTER 4

Contrary Evidence

It is an infallible rule that a prince who is not wise
himself cannot be well advised. . . .

MACHIAVELLI
The Prince

FAILURE AND SUCCESS: SOME DEFINITIONS

It is striking that virtually none of the participants or commentators on university-based attempts to advise local governments whom we have quoted to this point felt it necessary to specify what they meant by failure or success. There are probably two reasons for this. The first is that we have not here been considering the outcomes of basic research or the utility of knowledge. Were those the questions, it would have been obvious that "success" might assume many forms and arise in many degrees. It would have taken a nice discrimination operating against clear criteria, therefore, before any flat judgment of failure or success could confidently have been pronounced. Here, instead, we are considering advice—findings or conclusions sought by (or on behalf of) an urban client, with the expectation that they have some practical use. The tests to be applied to such efforts are somewhat more straightforward. Secondly, the "failures" described to this point have typically failed by any commonsense standard; they had no substantial redeeming virtue.

Nonetheless, as we now begin to examine more closely what we mean by success and failure and what factors seem to account for one or the other, it will be useful to draw some distinctions.

Advice to local officials is normally intended to meet one or more of three needs:*

1. *Identifying the problem.* Advice may assess the nature or seriousness of a problem and (or) identify its cause. In either case, it describes but does not propose. An example is the Urban Observatory study of Denver's economic base.

2. *Proposing the solution.* Starting either from his own findings or those of others as to the nature and cause of a problem, the adviser may propose a solution or alternative solutions and perhaps offer a basis for comparing the alternatives. The Stony Brook study of sanitation work schedules—up to the point at which the analyst was assigned to clear away objections to a test—is an example.

3. *Getting there from here.* An adviser may submit a plan for implementing a proposal. But more commonly, advice on ac-

---

*Obviously, there are less straightforward reasons for seeking (or offering) advice. These include using the advising process to defer action while seeming to act; to strengthen public support for a policy already chosen; to avoid or share responsibility for the course proposed; to coopt the advisers for other purposes; and no doubt others. On the offering side, a desire for public exposure, a need to supplement income, the hope of stimulating other contracts may be the underlying ends. But questions of motivation need not long entangle us. Whatever the "real" reason (or, more probably, the real mixture of reasons) for seeking advice, the outcome of the request is almost always intended to be one of the objects above. That appears especially true at the local level, where governments' responsibilities are operational and immediate, and the public believes that issues are simple enough to be understood and resolved without much hand wringing.

complishing change is provided through the adviser's participation in the effort to put a proposal into effect. Here, advice begins to border on direct assistance. The involvement of the Stony Brook analyst in testing the new sanitation work schedule is an example.

On the face of it, the standards against which to measure advising relationships are simple and the same for each case: did the client get what it expected and the adviser promised? But for many of these relationships, marked as they were by third-party backers and poorly specified objectives, those intentions are difficult to identify. So it seems useful to establish some presumptive intentions or standard tests of success. The tests will vary according to the purpose of the advice.

Advice intended simply to identify a problem is meant to explain. It can reasonably be regarded as successful, therefore, to exactly the extent that the explanation is objectively accurate. Proposed solutions, however, are normally intended as bases for action. They can be regarded as successful, therefore, only to the extent they are implementable, at least in principle. That is, they should be both objectively responsive to the problem and apparently capable of being acted upon by the client or intended beneficiary of the advice. Advice on implementation should probably meet the stiffest test. Since its purpose is to help actually to accomplish change, it should be regarded as successful only to the extent that the change intended is in fact accomplished.

Armed with these standards, we will look again at the experience of academics and officials described in the preceding chapters. But first we seek perspective by looking elsewhere—mainly at the experience of the many institutions other than universities which, during the 1960s and early 1970s, also sought to advise city governments.

The Professional Consultants

Universities were hardly the only suppliers of advice to city governments. Commercial management consulting firms, the analytic arms of manufacturing corporations, federally-oriented nonprofit research institutions, ad hoc locally-based consulting organizations, various state leagues and national associations, and many individuals also sought to provide usable advice to city governments. For our purposes, the most interesting of these providers are the professional management consulting firms.

In 1940, there were roughly 400 management consulting firms in the United States. By 1970, the number exceeded 3,000. The new industry employed some 60,000 people, and it performed substantial work for government as well as for private clients. More than one-third of the 1973 revenues of Booz, Allen and Hamilton, for example, were derived from federal, state, and local governments. The record of the consulting firms in dealing with city governments is interesting here for two reasons. First, they were more intensively used by local governments than any other source of technical or managerial advice: the 1970 survey by the International City Management Association cited earlier traced the sources of advice to 280 cities on questions of science or technology and found that 60 percent utilized advice from colleges or universities; 39 percent, from industry and business; 64 percent, from national associations; 60 percent, from the state leagues; and 88 percent, from private consulting firms.[1] And more importantly, the provision of advice to clients was the sole profession of these firms. If their work for city governments was markedly less successful than that for other clients, a reasonable inference would be that city agencies may be particularly difficult clients to help.

We shall examine five of the most substantial (and best documented) relationships between city governments and several varieties of professional consultants.

PITTSBURGH REVISITED

In chapter 2 we have already touched on the history of one relationship between a city government and a private consulting firm: the firm was CONSAD; the city, Pittsburgh. A new and relatively small organization and with no prior experience in urban policy making, CONSAD found the technical challenge of model building (for which it was well qualified) attractive, and either failed to understand or wholly ignored the almost certain uselessness of its emerging products for their only public purpose—namely to predict the consequences of alternative policies with sufficient accuracy to clarify the choice among them. Garry Brewer quotes a university-based participant in the effort as reporting:

They were good computer people, they knew what computers could do in training pilots, gaming and that sort of thing. But in terms of hard research results and in terms of policy making, I think they had the naive notion that because simulation, computer simulation, could do these other things it could also make policy and could produce research findings of very advanced types.[2]

As Brewer also demonstrates, CONSAD's behavior encountered no external discipline. Neither CONSAD's university co-workers nor Pittsburgh's own officials possessed the will or capacity to effectively monitor its work, and neither anticipated, until very late, that the extraordinarily ambitious simulation model which CONSAD undertook to build could not be relied upon to help resolve any substantial issues Pittsburgh faced. The unfamiliarity of Pittsburgh's planning officials with consulting relationships was compounded in this case by the highly technical and sophisticated techniques the consultant was applying.

The lesson of this story is at least equivocal. On the one hand, the consultant, by any reasonable standard, behaved poorly. CONSAD produced a product almost certain to fail at its intended purpose. On the other hand, the overselling of goods and services by their producers is hardly unfamiliar. And where a complex product is intended to meet standards never achieved before, high costs, delays in delivery, and unreliable performance are routine. A city government which contracts for such a product without acquiring the competence to understand or evaluate it—to say nothing of contributing to its development and use—is hardly blameless. Indeed, the client here was unable even to specify what it wanted. A former Pittsburgh planning official distributed responsibility this way:

> There are a hell of a lot of people who are charlatans of the first water, and they have exhibited it in this kind of undertaking. They have gone out and grabbed contracts, didn't know what the hell they were doing, and learned at the expense of the client . . . in the case of (CONSAD), *as is the problem with most consultants that don't perform, their problem was their client.* [emphasis added][3]

A Pittsburgh politician derived a more operational lesson from the experience. "When I want to hire a consultant now," he remarked, "I give him a very narrow and specific task to do."[4] Other things being equal, narrow and specific tasks are easier to perform than broad and general ones. They are more likely to call for a familiar and tested expertise. They can also be more clearly described and more competently supervised.

ARTHUR D. LITTLE IN SAN FRANCISCO

Brewer's penetrating study dissects the work for another city government of a much larger, older, and more experienced consulting organization.

Arthur D. Little (ADL), a Cambridge, Massachusetts-based

firm founded in 1886, employed in the early 1960s a staff of more than 1,000 persons. It offered consulting services and advice concerning the development and use of new technology to many hundreds of private organizations and public agencies across the United States and abroad. Stimulated by prior conversations with ADL, the City Planning Department of San Francisco in 1962 sought and received federal funding for an ambitious CRP program. In the words of a 1963 ADL paper, the CRP would:

> . . . deal in an integrated fashion with all public and private actions which must be taken to provide continuous and sound maintenance and development of the City's land and buildings . . . it will include all government actions which affect urban physical change, planning together for maximum effect, and designed to eliminate gaps and overlaps in treatment. . . . When completed, the CRP will indicate the kinds of renewal actions that are needed, when specific renewal activities should be started (as a part of the total program), where such actions should be taken and by whom.[5]

Most of this information was to be produced through a large-scale computer simulation model. The effort to construct and operate that model ended some three years later, having produced nothing San Francisco could use. One observer's estimate was that "the city got about three cents on the dollar."[6] The problems were familiar ones.

Though ADL was an experienced and competent firm, it had never produced as complex a simulation model for an urban client as it had promised San Francisco. Its San Francisco office, moreover, had been oriented principally to the physical sciences and had no experience in urban planning. But the firm sensed that the ambitious CRP was a major opportunity; large-scale computer-based urban decision models might be the wave of the future. In Brewer's words, ADL had "an institutional stake in the CRP as a means to create an able reputation in an expanding segment of the consultants business. . . ."[7]

Here again, and not unnaturally, a consultant was inclined to take on an enormously complex project for which it had little expertise and no direct experience. Here again, the inclination met no challenge from the intended client. The financing arrangements were one powerful reason why. Under the standard CRP funding formula, the federal Housing and Home Financing Agency required San Francisco to "pay" one-third of the roughly one million dollars the program was to cost. But that contribution required little diversion of resources since the costs of existing city facilities and the salaries of current city employees could be counted as the municipal contribution. "Feeling little or no fiscal obligation," as Brewer observed:

the Board of Supervisors and the mayor had slight reason to appraise seriously the merits of the proposal as to the feasibility, method, or possible impact. Should the program go awry, the Board of Supervisors had a hedge and could always tell critics ". . . we never wanted this anyway. The only reason that we were sold on this is because it was free."[8]

Poor administration at the political level was compounded by politics at the administrative level. The city's Department of City Planning, loser of many bureaucratic fights with the local Urban Renewal Agency, saw a chance in the CRP to grab a promising piece of future action. It pressed for the federal grant, therefore, partly uncaring as well as partly unconscious of the demands which supervision of the effort would place upon itself. One consultant commented:

The Department of City Planning was as naive at times as you could possibly encounter anywhere. They had what I would call the "pin ball machine syndrome." They were fascinated by bright colored lights and prestige considerations and they had no clear idea of how they wanted to use this thing.[9]

The remainder of the story is predictable. ADL quickly realized that the comprehensive land use model originally proposed for the entire bay area was vastly more complex than could be produced. It retreated to the more modest objective of a model of San Francisco residential housing stock, designed so that it still might assist in the making of city policy. But much of the requisite data was nonexistent or unavailable (two city agencies declined to open their files), and the scope of the model contracted again. Though repeatedly narrowed in purpose, the model continued to impose extraordinary conceptual and methodological problems. These could be solved only through a series of questionable assumptions and simplifications, and resort to demographic data inadequate to the levels of precision to which the model pretended. Even had its logic been sound, the model, because it purported to describe changes in population and housing stock in very small areas of the city, required data more detailed and more accurate than existed. As a result, when the model's eventual outputs disagreed with the educated instincts of the officials who were shown them, there was no basis for defending those outputs as more accurate or useful than unaided judgment.

From 1965 to 1968 attempts were made to correct and adjust the model. Given time enough and funding, these might have produced a modestly useful device. But by 1968, personnel turnover in both the Department of City Planning and in ADL, successive changes in the scope and purpose of the model, and shifting of the city's policy interests had produced too many discontinuities. Said the planning director,

"To the extent that it *could* answer questions, they were questions that nobody was asking."[10] The effort was abandoned.

THE NEW YORK EXPERIENCE

John Lindsay was elected mayor of New York City in 1965 with what appeared to be a mandate for reform. The city was clearly in trouble: the middle class moving to the suburbs, the welfare case load growing, the city's economy uncertain, and all indices of social decay—crime, building abandonment, fire alarms—on the rise. New York's bureaucracy was huge (almost 400,000 employees), still growing, and widely regarded as cumbersome, inefficient, and rooted in archaic work patterns.

Lindsay was determined to challenge old policies, reassess traditional practices, and reorganize the government. He gathered some fifty functionally-related but previously independent bureaus and agencies together under common direction in a small group of "superagencies"—Health and Hospitals, Human Resources, Environmental Protection. He recruited energetic (though generally inexperienced) new administrators. He used the city's extensively restaffed Budget Bureau to rethink objectives, to design new programs, and to force-feed change to the agencies—roles that accorded poorly with the bureau's accustomed functions as monitor of performance and guardian of the purse. He required almost all agencies to inaugurate comprehensive Planning, Programming, and Budgeting (PPB) systems modeled on the procedures by which Robert McNamara's Defense Department had related its budget requests to major policy objectives rather than to accounting categories. He forced the development, in each major agency, of an internal analytic and planning staff. And to help rethink the city's policies and to review its operations, he brought to bear a wide variety of research and consulting organizations.

The work of the major outside consultants, stimulated and controlled by the Budget Bureau, was by American municipal standards well directed and relatively productive. But it was also risky and uncertain. Both truths are reflected in a remark of David Grossman, successively deputy director and director of the Budget Bureau: "Fifty percent of our consulting money was wasted. I was terribly proud of that. No other city was doing nearly so well."[11]

We look here at the city's experience with two of its major consultants, the RAND Corporation, and McKinsey and Company.

THE NEW YORK CITY–RAND INSTITUTE

Unlike CONSAD, The RAND Corporation was large and well established—indeed the model and archetype of the independent government-oriented "think tank." Unlike ADL, RAND was not hard-technology oriented (it maintained no laboratories). Unlike McKinsey, it was a nonprofit institution limited to work "in the public interest"; it took no private or commercial clients.

RAND had been created by the U.S. Air Force in the late 1940s. It had provided a setting in which the civilian scientists and strategists who had served the Air Corps in World War II could be retained to address the unfamiliar uncertainties of cold war, nuclear weapons, and rapidly changing technology. RAND had been consciously designed to meet a distinctive set of criteria: concern for policy studies rather than either basic or low-level applied research; sufficient assurance of continued funding to provide independence; a research charter broad enough to permit analysts to follow a problem wherever it led them; an internal environment that encouraged analysts from various disciplines to work jointly; and a broad "systems" approach.[12] None of these qualities were characteristic of univer-

sity-based research organizations. Yet their possession by
RAND, central to its effectiveness with federal clients, was no
guarantee of success in New York.

Late in 1967, Mayor Lindsay and Budget Director Frederick
O'R. Hayes asked the RAND Corporation to assist in the
analysis and reform of a number of city agencies. Though based
in California and without experience in work for local government, RAND had already begun to address domestic social
issues and was attracted by Lindsay's strong interest. After
some months of discussion, RAND agreed to undertake studies
of New York's police procedures, fire protection, and health
and housing issues; and as those studies proceeded, RAND
accepted additional contracts for work on problems of water
pollution, criminal correction, welfare, and the New York City
labor market.

By the spring of 1969, some thirty separate studies were
underway. They were being staffed by roughly forty RAND
analysts, most of them bright, young, and well trained in economics, regional planning, or the hard sciences. Virtually none
had worked in or with a city government before. By the summer of 1969 the relation of the city government and RAND
seemed sufficiently promising to justify transforming RAND's
New York office into a new institution, and the New York
City–RAND Institute (NYC–RI) was established. Essentially
a joint venture of RAND and the city government, the institute was a nonprofit corporation, staffed and administered by
RAND, subject to the oversight of a board of trustees chosen
jointly by RAND and the city, and designed to work continu-
ously on issues of concern to New York. The institute was a
substantial enterprise and well supported; its annual budgets of
some $2.5 million were made up principally of city funds,
augmented by a three-year $900,000 Ford Foundation grant
and several federal grants and contracts. The institute was
intended to be independent enough to be critical of city poli-

cies, sufficiently insulated from the city's daily operating concerns to address underlying problems but close enough in its working relations with city agencies to produce timely, realistic, and usable recommendations. Because it was created and designed expressly to provide usable policy advice and expertise to a city government, the institute's history is particularly instructive. And since the relations of the institute to the city's government have been better documented than those of any other urban adviser, the lessons of the experience can be drawn with somewhat greater confidence.[13]

The great range in the nature and outcome of the institute's efforts can be fairly represented through its work for six agencies.

Modeling a Bay. In 1968, New York's Department of Water Resources was considering where along the margins of Jamaica Bay to locate new sewage disposal and treatment plants and what capacities the plants would need. But traditional methods of analysis, dependent largely on physical models, could not determine what difference the choices of location and capacity would make to the water quality of the Bay. Jan Leendertse, a Dutch-born RAND expert in tidal flows and computer modeling, considered the city's problem and concluded that a computer-based simulation of the Bay could be designed to determine those effects. The city's water commissioner, an experienced engineer, understood the promise of the simulation but declined to fund so speculative an effort. RAND concluded, however, that the concept was feasible and that Leendertse could make it work; it therefore supported initial development of the model with its own funds.

A year's development produced a promising model. The water commissioner then not only authorized future funding but ordered the special collection of data to facilitate testing the model. Within two years, the model's increasingly refined projections agreed so closely with observed conditions that the

city was consulting it for guidance not only as to sewer treatment choices, but for a possible extension of Kennedy Airport
runways into the bay, the proposed construction by the Corps
of Engineers of a hurricane barrier across an inlet to the bay,
and for dredging and landfill questions. Beyond proving operationally useful to New York, Leendertse's work established a
powerful new analytic method of broad application. Models
adapted from that of Jamaica Bay are now routinely used by
the Corps of Engineers, several other U.S. coastal cities, and
the government of the Netherlands. The conjunction of a
demanding and knowledgeable client with a researcher whose
particular skill matched the client's problem (and of a research
institute willing to invest its own funds in a speculative enterprise) produced a clear success. A problem was not only solved
in principle but worked out in operational detail. And the
solution was incorporated into routine practice not only by the
client but by others.

A Failure in Health.   RAND's work for the city's Health
Services Administration (HSA) was of a very different character. Except for the Veterans Administration, HSA was the
largest publicly-supported health agency in the nation. But
only recently established, incorporating the previously autono-
mous departments of Health, Hospitals, and Mental Health,
it was wracked by internal conflict, harried by rapidly-rising
costs, and weakened by rapid turnover of key personnel. Into
that setting, institute researchers were introduced through the
powerful sponsorship of the Budget Bureau acting for the
mayor. But obliged to respond to officials rapidly replaced by
others, inexperienced both in medicine and in medical administration, and regarded by many as agents of the Budget
Bureau, the analysts found it difficult to identify tractable
issues on which HSA staffs were interested in having them
work.

A fair fraction of the institute's work proved modestly useful

in the Health and Mental Health Departments, two component agencies whose deputy commissioners invested considerable effort in using RAND and in focusing its efforts. For
example, RAND's suggestions for reducing the high incidence
of lead poisoning of children (due apparently to ingestion of
lead-based paint from peeling walls) were adopted by the
Health Department and transformed into its own formal proposal to the Budget Bureau. (No action resulted, however, for
reasons of cost.) Similarly, the institute's specification of those
areas of the city with greatest mental health problems established a base for the city's subsequent mental health planning.
In neither case had sophisticated research methods been used.
And in both cases the studies had merely demonstrated what
some officials in the department had "known" all along. But
instinctive "knowledge" could not document the case for policy change; the analyses could.

Work for other components of HSA almost uniformly
failed, however, and attempts to provide usable staff work
directly to the successive administrators of HSA were a
source of great frustration to both parties. One reason for the
failures was that HSA had begun to develop its own central
staff of analysts, and that staff came to view the RAND analysts as competitors. A succession of HSA clients, moreover,
were put off by RAND's reluctance to work on unrelated
low-level issues. "I insisted they work on short-term analyses.
. . . But RAND continued to try to do the global and impossible things, like overall cost-effectiveness of our health programs,"[14] remarked one HSA official. Institute researchers
were willing to establish their bona fides by working on some
issues they regarded as minor, but they also worried that larger
issues of municipal health policy were being ignored. As the
senior RAND health analyst complained, "The city is too
concerned with next week and not one, two, or three years
ahead. . . . Throughout all this I've had the feeling we've

been grooming a mastodon about to walk over a cliff."[15]

Over the course of three years, the institute's health project produced more than sixty studies and cost some $1.75 million. The descriptive studies can be accounted generally successful; their assessments were largely accurate. Very little advice on implementation was attempted. The large number of studies proposing solutions or courses of action typically met one standard—they were technically competent analyses—but failed another: they could not be implemented. A good example was one of the ten analyses to address a major policy question: did New York need additional hospitals? The study showed that city hospitals already possessed excess capacity, that systems for better utilization of existing beds could readily be designed, and that in terms of medical needs, the construction of the new hospitals then being planned was almost certainly an enormously expensive mistake. The analysis was correct, but the pressures on the city government to continue hospital construction were too powerful to be contained by the results of analysis. The construction program continued.

Fire Fighting.   The institute's most effective and most enduring work was performed for (and with) New York City's Fire Department. A traditional agency, conservative by temperament, and resistant to change, the fire department was under enormous pressure in the late 1960s. Alarm rates had more than tripled in five years, and false alarms were rising even faster. Fire companies housed in areas of high fire incidence were being ground down by unsustainable work loads. But the city's budgetary squeeze precluded simple expansion of the department.

As had been true for HSA, the fire department had no choice but to enter a relationship with RAND: the mayor's office required that much. But the question of what issues would be addressed, and how, was open. After initial skepticism, an energetic and newly-appointed fire chief supported the RAND connection, involved himself deeply in the choice of subjects to be analyzed, and assigned subordinates to work actively with the RAND researchers. Operating in parallel with the chief was an experienced civilian analyst placed in the department at Budget Bureau insistence. His interest lay in seeing analyses produce useful change, and he had no substantial staff of his own to compete with the institute's analysts.

A bit of luck intruded early. The leader of the institute's fire project, a chemical engineer, was aware that minute amounts of long-chain polymers reduce turbulence in the flow of liquids. He arranged a series of demonstrations that showed how controlled injections of such polymers into a firehose stream quite substantially increased both the amount of water the hoses could supply and the distance the stream could carry from the nozzle. This "slippery water" (or "Rapid Water" as the proud commercial supplier of the polymer redubbed it) required some detailed engineering to make it feasible; getting the polymers mixed into the hose stream in correct proportions required special pumps. Nonetheless, it was clear from the first tests that the novelty would work, and it became clear shortly thereafter that it promised benefits to all parties. The mayor, photographed at the demonstrations, got credit for introducing some of the innovation his campaign had promised. Senior managers of the fire department, along with budget officials, foresaw a growth in fire-fighting capacity without increased budgets. The firemen's union shortly thereafter realized that the greater water-flow could make possible the use of smaller-diameter hose, which was lighter, safer, and easier to control. Dow Chemical supported the necessary engineering work in anticipation of both a new market and credit for responding to a growing big city problem. The result was that the succeeding years saw New York's pumpers all gradually equipped to use "Rapid Water" and the spread of the new technology to several other cities as well. "Rapid Water" was uncharacteristic of the kind of assistance RAND offered the fire department, but it immediately established RAND's credentials and provided a grace period during which less spectacular but more important innovations could be developed.

Another early study examined the department's dispatching centers. Dispatchers were required to decide with great speed which units to send to new alarms. But in doing so they had to take a great deal into account: the status of units already engaged elsewhere, the position of other companies relocated to cover areas of the city whose units were committed to fires in progress, and the probable duration and intensity both of fires in progress and those precipitating the new alarms. On particularly busy nights, those judgments became harder—and slower—to make; substantial delays in dispatching were becoming common. The department's idea was to computerize the process. A small RAND group spent months closely observing the dispatching problems and then built a simple simulation model. The analysts concluded that a solution far cheaper than computers was preferable: simply dividing responsibility for busy boroughs between two dispatchers. For two years, factions in the department resisted that conclusion. But sustained testing, adaptation, and persuasion, pressed on the department by a persistent and committed researcher, eventually brought the new system into operation, and it proved a great success.[16]

The central work of the institute's fire project involved the building of a much more complex simulation model designed to test the effect of alternative locations of new fire houses and of alternative strategies for responding to fires. One of the model's early findings was that a so-called "adaptive response" —the dispatching, in response to alarms unlikely to represent structural fires, of fewer units than the traditional three pumpers and two ladder trucks—would greatly decrease work overloads and actually improve protection across the city. The strategy was simple, and it had often been suggested; the virtue of this work was not originality but an authoritative showing that the reform would prove safe and effective. The model also provided a basis for much else: changes in duty hours to make manning rates conform more closely to predictable patterns of fire incidence; determining appropriate locations for new fire-fighting companies; and developing a management information and control system far more sophisticated than any U.S. fire department had previously operated. The ultimate effect of the modeling was not only to make the department's work far more "cost effective" but slowly to transform the department's understanding of the management function. By showing how innovations too risky for operational experiment could be tested through computer simulation, it drew both department officials and officers of the firemen's union into more coherent and rigorous discussion of alternative methods of operation than had been possible before.

The institute's work with the fire department was, therefore, successful even by the most demanding of tests: virtually all of it proved not only technically proficient but usable, and when put into effect—with substantial help from the institute—it had clearly beneficial results. Some of the sources of that success seem clear. As one review concluded:

The Fire Department's operations were well documented, easily quantified, and had unambiguous objectives, making them an ideal subject of RAND's modeling techniques. . . . Second, the department's managers, faced with serious and complex problems of administration, were already convinced that they could not continue to conduct business as usual. . . . Finally, the organizational arrangements of the RAND Institute itself and the kind of connection that its research team managed to establish with the Fire Department helped the analysts exploit the advantages that were offered by the department's distinctive organizational characteristics.[17]

That connection between RAND and the department was hardly free of conflict, but it remained close, collegial, and productive. RAND analysts spent much of their time at departmental headquarters or in fire houses or dispatching centers. Models were developed with the active involvement of fire officials and, to a limited extent, of union representatives. Key personnel on both sides of the relationship remained in place for some years. And one important change in personnel told much about the relationship. When the analyst first employed by the department left to become a deputy police commissioner, his replacement, selected by the fire commissioner and fire chief, was a senior RAND staff member.

Human Resources.   The institute's work for New York City's Human Resources Administration (HRA) and for its Police Department had oddly similar histories—of initial rejection, strong recoveries, and then termination.

From the beginning of RAND's presence in New York City both the mayor and the Budget Bureau were eager for the institute to address the manifold problems of the Human Resources Administration. The city's welfare population had tripled between 1963 and 1968, and HRA's soaring budget was the largest of any city department. The department strained under its gigantic caseload, its accounting systems were suspect, and relations with welfare recipients were poor and deteriorating. But in 1968 the HRA administrator noted that RAND had no relevant previous experience, suspected that it might seek to serve the mayor's office rather than HRA, and declined to accept its help. Nor was RAND eager to take HRA on as a client. For several years, at Budget Bureau insistence, RAND reluctantly performed some modest analytic and managerial tasks for HRA, but little of value was accomplished and relations among all the parties were strained.

The situation remained unchanged until 1971, when HRA appointed a new deputy administrator who had effectively used

RAND analysts in his previous position with the city's housing agency. He began by assembling a competent internal office of policy research. Jointly, staff members of the policy research office and the institute then designed and began major studies of the economic and demographic factors influencing caseload growth, of the circumstances which distinguished welfare from nonwelfare poor, and of the effectiveness of the city's job training programs in reducing welfare dependency. The studies proved helpful. They gave HRA a method of anticipating changes in caseload and consequently of improving its own budgetary and personnel projections; they produced a proposal for rationalizing the erratic patterns of welfare benefits, and they sharply enhanced the agency's understanding of the dynamics of poverty in the city. Still, the department possessed so little control over the demands upon it that the analyses had little immediate operational impact. Had the new RAND–HSA relationship been sustained, they might have had an effect but, as will be described, all institute work for the city was to end in 1975.

A Stand-off with the Police. RAND found the New York City Police Department even more difficult to work for. Insular, traditionally suspicious of outsiders, all the more defensive in 1968 because of criticisms of police brutality and the attempted intervention by young assistants of the mayor in tactical police operations, the department did not welcome RAND.

Unlike his HRA counterpart, however, the police commissioner accepted a contract with RAND. A broad, well-funded work program was agreed upon, its content largely reflecting Budget Bureau interests rather than those of the police department. The institute began a number of small-scale analyses— of recruitment and training, the department's responses to charges of misconduct, the operations of the detective bureau, and the effectiveness of uniformed versus nonuniformed patrol. It also undertook a more ambitious analysis of how officers might be deployed to better match, in time and place, the probable need for them.

But relations between the department and RAND remained less than cordial. No ranking police official sought to guide or advise the analysts, some elements of the department declined to cooperate with institute staffers, and few relations of trust or confidence developed. None arose at higher levels. Moreover, a number of the issues the institute was exploring were of high political or bureaucratic sensitivity. The deployment studies threatened long-established work routines. The review of the handling of citizen complaints appeared likely to produce highly critical findings not long after a bitter fight over a civilian review board had ended, and the institute's recommendations for reorganizing the detective bureau touched inadvertently on one of the most explosive internal rivalries in the department. A year and a half after signing the original contract with RAND, the police commissioner, for reasons he refused to specify, declined to renew the institute's contract.

As it happened, a new commissioner, known as a reformer, was appointed in 1970. Without immediately reestablishing relations with the institute, he nonetheless began drawing on the now considerable volume of RAND studies of New York City police operations. The detective division was reorganized, for the first time in fifty years, along the lines RAND had proposed. Changes in the department's handling of civilian complaints were also instituted, again in accordance with RAND recommendations. By 1972, the department had again become a client of the institute. A more modest set of studies reflecting the commissioner's interests were begun by a new set of institute staffers. Liaison with the department was attended to more carefully, and the institute added to its staff a retired senior police official. But relations between RAND researchers and working levels in the department remained distant, impediments to innovation in the department remained formidable, and few additional changes in policy or in operations had been achieved before RAND's work for the city came to an end.

Reforming Rent Control. In terms of magnitude of effect, the institute's most important work was performed for the city's Housing and Development Administration.

The work began unpromisingly, with sharp disagreement between housing officials and institute staff as to what needed doing. Virtually all city officials believed that the central problem was how to reduce the time, capital, and administrative energy required to produce new publicly-assisted housing. The period between acquisition of land and the moving in of a first tenant was approaching a decade, construction costs were rising through the levels of federal assistance ceilings, construction targets were not being met, and clamor for additional housing was increasing rapidly. The analysts, they thought, should explore new construction technologies and develop new production-management techniques. After some initial uncertainty, the analysts concluded otherwise. As Ira Lowry, the leader of the RAND work, later wrote:

We came to believe that the attention of City officials should be focused on saving the existing stock from the growing threat of deterioration and abandonment, and that solutions must be sought on a City-wide scale. While the specific problems and fears associated with ethnic turnover were critical factors in the decay of some neighborhoods, the more pervasive problem was that most owners of the controlled housing were not getting enough revenue to maintain their buildings properly and still earn a reasonable return on capital. [The city still maintained a system of rent control first adopted during World War II; it covered about half the tenants in the city.] The issue that was least clear was the extent to which these revenue shortages were directly due to rent control, as distinguished from the poverty of the tenants.

We launched or provided technical assistance in a number of

studies designed to probe and test these views. By 1969, we were sure
we had a case and began to formulate a strategy. . . .

We recommended raising ceiling rents to cover standard full costs,
much in the pattern of public-utility rate-setting; a program of direct
rent assistance to low-income families to offset the rent increases;
improved code enforcement as a check on landlord delinquency; and
a special program addressed to persistently substandard buildings,
involving systematic diagnosis of the reasons for delinquency and the
use of a wide range of treatment options. We provided estimates of
program impacts and program costs.

It was a long, hard, selling job. . . . Every critical comment by
someone whose opinion carried weight in administration circles
sent us back to the drawing board. Some disagreed with our diagnosis, or at least questioned whether our evidence was robust. Others
were satisfied with the diagnosis but doubted the adequacy of our
remedies. Others accepted their adequacy but questioned their administrative or fiscal or political feasibility. In particular, our
proposals to tamper with the system of rent control so as to raise
rents to cover supply costs were regarded by most as politically impossible.

That our proposals concerning rent control were eventually accepted by the HDA, the Bureau of the Budget, and finally by the
Mayor's Office is due to a combination of . . . factors:

—Our arguments were . . . forcefully presented in a steady flow
of briefings and documents.

—Our principal liaison with the agency was heavily committed to
the enterprise and worked with tremendous energy and skill to advance the cause within the agency.

—The visible symptoms of trouble in the housing market increased and intensified throughout this period, so that the issues
raised by our work continued to command official attention.

The existing rent control statute was due to expire at the end of
March 1970, unless renewed by the City Council. As the winter wore
on, the counterpolemics of landlord and tenant organizations became
even more extravagant than usual. The City Council, the press, and
the public began to demand that the administration reveal its plans.
The New York Times acquired a bundle of draft material that had

been circulated within the IIDA, including portions of our work, from which it quoted selectively in a series of news stories. The City Council demanded access to this mysterious document; one group of Councilmen sued HDA for its release.[18]

The institute study was released to the council and intensive negotiations began between the mayor's office and council members. RAND staff took no direct role but were periodically asked to trace the consequences of various alternative provisions of the new law. In June 1970, the council enacted a substantial reform modeled closely on the RAND proposal. Its basic principle was that the level of controlled rents would be based not on arbitrary adjustments to the rents in effect when control had begun twenty-seven years before, but on the current cost of providing well-maintained housing.

Much work remained to be done, and it proved exceedingly difficult. Formulas were developed to calculate the costs of maintaining housing of various types, but they required masses of data. Much of the information was hard to obtain and some precipitated sharp disagreement between landlords and tenants. Far simpler calculations, therefore, had to be substituted. The terms of the law, moreover, were altered by subsequent state legislation which wholly decontrolled apartments once they became vacant. But the achievement had been significant. A politically astute housing administrator, backed by an innovation-minded mayor and supported by an effective manager of research, had produced a politically difficult but fundamental reform. And the reform was based directly on the conclusions of a large, well-focused and well-integrated research program.* One skeptical but well-informed city official characterized RAND's contribution this way:

---

*Professor George Sternlieb of Rutgers University, as well as McKinsey and Company, had conducted significant supplementary studies.

RAND gave us several things we didn't have but needed. Most important, they brought a sophistication in statistical techniques we didn't have in the city. RAND did the careful analysis of census data to document the case for rent control changes of a major order. Second, RAND put its prestigious name behind drastic overhaul—and this was important in view of the tremendous political inertia over doing anything to change the situation. Finally, RAND conceived the notion of adjusting rents upwards by a formula which takes into account the changing costs of operating sound housing; before, it was on a case-by-case basis, the benefits were unevenly spread, and there was absolutely no logic to the situation. RAND didn't invent the policy of drastic change in rent control—many people had come to this conclusion, and the Mayor was predisposed to give it favorable consideration. But what RAND did do was to document the case more convincingly and thoroughly than anyone had ever done before.[19]

Termination. But four days after the council's enactment of the rent control reforms, City Comptroller Abraham Beame stopped payment on all the city's consultant contracts, including RAND's. During the previous month a series of front-page articles in the *New York Times* had argued that the widespread use of consulting by the Lindsay administration had permitted waste and fraud, arrogated to outsiders functions that were properly the province of civil servants, and amounted to little more than a novel form of patronage. Lindsay was a Republican. The majority of city council members were Democrats, as was Comptroller Beame, whom Lindsay had narrowly defeated in the mayoral race of 1965. The council had particular reason to resent the mayor's use of consultants since the administration had prepared for the battle over rent reform—the central political issue of that year—through the extensive use of its consultants but had denied the council access to their work. And the assertions about displacement of civil servants had great political appeal in a city of powerful government unions concerned somewhat about displacement but greatly about the consultants as allies of an antibureaucratic mayor.

Both the city council and the comptroller, therefore, took the position that no substantial consultant contracts could be awarded simply at the discretion of mayoral agencies. To back that decision the comptroller refused to consider for payment a large number of consulting contracts, including those of the institute. The dispute that followed took a year to make its way through the courts and the New York State Legislature, and at its conclusion, the position of the council and comptroller was upheld.

During the year of uncertainty, the institute, denied funding from the city, continued its major research efforts on a reduced level by drawing on internal RAND funding and foundation grants. By late 1971 it managed to secure city reimbursement for most of those efforts. Thus the institute survived, but the environment in which it worked had changed sharply. All consultant contracts were now politically vulnerable, especially as the city's financial circumstances became more difficult, and all had to be approved in advance by political opponents of the mayor. Under the new rules, RAND's work for some agencies (HRA, police) actually improved in power and utility, but other contracts were cancelled, most were reduced in scope, and the staff of the institution shrank. Then, in 1973, as the city's financial troubles continued to worsen, former Comptroller Beame became mayor. Some agencies—particularly the fire department—fought to retain their RAND connection and succeeded, but the contraction of the institute continued and in 1975 RAND closed it down; the few surviving projects were conducted for city agencies from RAND's main offices in Santa Monica.

MCKINSEY & COMPANY

The Lindsay administration drew upon McKinsey & Company almost as intensively as it did upon RAND. One of the oldest, largest, and most prestigious of U.S. management consulting firms, McKinsey by the late 1960s was engaged in a worldwide practice, and though most of its clients were commercial or industrial firms, it had performed substantial work for state and federal agencies.

McKinsey's home office was in New York City, and one of its senior partners, serving in 1967 as a member of one of the several voluntary advisory committees established by the Lindsay administration, offered the mayor's Policy Planning Council a demonstration of a technique McKinsey called "issue mapping." Through a sequence of carefully worked out wall-sized charts, issue mapping provided a clear visual guide through the logic of a complex policy problem. It proceeded in the same way that any competent written analysis would. It defined a problem, identified its causes, suggested alternative solutions, and made explicit the criteria (of cost, probable effectiveness, speed, political acceptability, and the like) against which the alternatives could be measured. In this period of the Lindsay administration, when major decisions were regularly being debated in the Policy Planning Council, the great virtue of issue mapping was that it provided continuous visual reference points for the progress of a debate. Whether led by the McKinsey partner who had prepared the issue maps or by a member of the council, the discussion could be guided through a logical progression, from symptoms to causes to possible cures, with all participants focused on the same points as the argument proceeded. The charts helped to channel discussion and to clarify where the group agreed, where it disagreed, and why.

Impressed with the device and with Carter Bales, the young McKinsey partner who had presented it, the council contracted with McKinsey for issue mapping studies of at least four policy problems. Payment for the work was to be $50,000, well under McKinsey's cost for a single professional man-year. McKinsey accepted the contract, partly from a sense of public responsibility, partly from a desire to demonstrate its capacity to deal with public policy issues, and partly from an interest in recruiting the ablest young business-school graduates who, like their law-school colleagues of those years, were eager to engage in "public interest" work.

The results were predictable. Though McKinsey committed great talent and energy to the work, and though the study teams were filled out by young analysts from the mayor's office, the time and resources available did not permit authoritative work on so wide a range of complex issues. The first product of the contract, an analysis of alternative approaches to air pollution abatement, was comprehensive and sophisticated— a "virtuoso performance," as Frederick O'R. Hayes called it. But as Hayes allowed, "None of the succeeding issue maps reached the same exalted level," even though McKinsey committed to the effort more than three times the professional manpower its fee could pay for.[20]

Still, the issue mapping experience produced a number of useful effects. It provided city officials with several excellent models of how policy analysis should be done. It built good working relationships among the younger urban-oriented members of the McKinsey staff and the analysts of similar background whom Lindsay and Hayes had been seeding through the city government. And, at least among the mayor's associates, it stimulated a taste for further attempts to bring the analytic techniques of modern business management to bear on the city's weaknesses in policy making and administration.

As a result, in 1968, Hayes asked Carter Bales to lead the introduction of planning-programming-budgeting (PPB) systems throughout city government and gave him the title of assistant budget director to facilitate the work. At the same time, McKinsey assumed a number of other tasks in Lindsay's program of renovating New York City's government. Through a variety of contacts with elements of the mayor's office and with line agencies, it was soon engaged in attempting to push through management improvements in trash and garbage collection; designing methods to manage and monitor Model Cities programs; trying to anticipate the effects of school decentralization; and rationalizing the city's tax collection procedures. Most heroically, McKinsey, early in 1970, undertook a central role in designing the structure and operating procedures for a new Health and Hospitals Corporation, an agency designed to begin administering the city's eighteen municipal hospitals in July of that year.

McKinsey's performance of those tasks was cut short by the political dispute over the mayor's use of consultants that began in the summer of 1970, a dispute particularly damaging to the firm. McKinsey had paid the expenses of one of the mayor's cabinet members and his family at a conference the firm held at a resort outside the city; criticism of that practice was followed by an attack on Bales's position as involving a conflict of interest since the Budget Bureau supervised the awarding by city agencies of most consultant contracts. The expenses incident was a trivial transgression, and Bales's position, while irregular, had not been abused. But as the influence of the mayor's consultants became a political issue, both were embarrassing. And the pressures were compounded by the annoyance of some of McKinsey's corporate clients at the firm's involvement in the Lindsay proposals to raise taxes. Protective of its reputation, aware that the costs of its New York City work were exceeding income from the city by more than half a million dollars, and now apprehensive about the complexities of a political role, McKinsey sharply reduced and then ended its work for the city.

Abbreviated as the effort was, it permits a number of conclusions. Probably only two projects—those on sanitation and the tax system—can be accounted clearly successful. The first produced feasible proposals that led in fact to faster removal of abandoned cars, better maintenance of garbage trucks, and reduced waiting time in the unloading of trucks. The second, after further work by Budget Bureau staff, led to a pathbreaking system for accurately assessing the effects of revisions in the tax system on both the incidence of taxation and on total yields. In both cases, it is worth noting, the work was done for and with a well-led, competently staffed city agency seriously interested in a useful outcome.

In varying degrees, the other efforts were unproductive. The PPB design work required the major city agencies to provide demandingly detailed new bases for their budget requests and to accompany the requests with analyses of program effectiveness of a quality that few agencies had the capacity to perform. Requiring too much too soon, the system generated far more paperwork than insight. It was shortly abandoned. The second large-scale effort, the attempt to design an effective Health and Hospitals Corporation (HHC), was a more serious failure. Virtually none of the corporation's administrative or financial or personnel systems were ready for operation when the HHC came into being in the summer of 1970. As a result, its first years, difficult ones for any large new public enterprise, were plagued with confusion, conflict, and poor performance. But in these cases, the "client" agencies of the work were either hostile (PPB) or only marginally competent (hospitals); they lacked either the incentive or the capacity to use what McKinsey attempted to supply. Hayes's assessment of this history is that

> The PPB design work for budget was unrealistic in its anticipation of agency performance—a judgment for which I bear more than half the burden. The design work for the Hospital Corporation was disappointing for a multitude of reasons, including a sponsor of limited responsiveness and capacity, the shortcomings in the work of related consultants, but also, a poorly developed sense of strategy and perception in the McKinsey team.[21]

The larger lessons of McKinsey's experience are strikingly similar to those of RAND's. In both cases, working relationships were readily established with the innovation-minded political leadership of the new administration, but only painfully and partially with the bureaucracies which in the end would determine whether the innovations would be adopted and used or rejected. In both cases, consultant and client supposed that innovation could be achieved by supply-push rather than demand-pull, and in both cases, the strategy succeeded only where demand at the operating level could be found or (more rarely) induced. In both cases, the analytic outsiders, in their relations with the bureaucracy, had to overcome a number of disadvantages at once: their youth (at both McKinsey and RAND, the mean age of the analysts was under thirty and that of the project leaders was only a few years more); their unfamiliarity with the substantive work of their client agencies (the expertise behind RAND's work on water quality was a rare exception); and their close association with a political leadership regarded by municipal employees as antibureaucratic and antiunion.

And in both cases, the political system into which they had been introduced rejected the transplant. Neither RAND nor McKinsey (nor the mayor's office) understood early enough the degree to which the consultants had become politically significant and therefore liable to political attack. When the attack came, RAND and McKinsey discovered that the press was skeptical, the city council hostile, the municipal unions pleased at their come-uppance, the comptroller implacable. Their only supporter was the mayor, and he had little support to give.

LATS, MYSTIQUE IN SEARCH OF A MISSION

By the late 1960s, the technological strength and project management skills of the aerospace industry were widely admired. At the same time American cities in "crisis" needed help. Both new technologies and more effective management looked potentially helpful. And the aerospace market was contracting, putting engineers, systems analysts, and management specialists out of work. The conclusion was obvious—these talents ought now to be redeployed in the service of cities. That logic seemed most powerful in Southern California, center of the aerospace industry and site of its highest unemployment. It is not surprising, then, that in 1967 an organization of former aerospace planners and technicians was established in Los Angeles to address the problems of the city.

The organization was the Los Angeles Technical Services Corporation (LATS). Proposed by Los Angeles business figures in 1966 and supported by Mayor Yorty, LATS began operations when its first substantial funding was received (from the Ford Foundation) in the following year. Its professed objectives were extraordinarily broad:

. . . to enable the use of available scientific and technological resources and techniques at the local level and to carry out programs that improve the quality of the urban environment . . . developing a comprehensive understanding of the community and opportunities to improve its condition; improving the community's available ability to perceive the effect of international, national, regional, and local forces on local conditions; improving local governments' skill and organization, and increasing its ability to use resources of the private

sector in improvement programs; improving related university cur-
ricula and research . . . and developing greater understanding of
community problems and problem-solving mechanisms within business and industry . . .[22]

In practice it confined itself to attempting to provide systematic planning or advanced technology to Los Angeles's municipal bureaucracies. That proved a difficult assignment.

LATS's Model Cities work was relatively successful. After a
Model Cities application prepared by the Los Angeles Public
Works Department was rejected by HUD, LATS organized a
new application group and produced a clearer, more comprehensive, and more ambitious plan. HUD approved and funded
it. But like those for many Model Cities, the plan proved
inconsistent and, in part, infeasible. Having perhaps foreseen
its problems, LATS took no part in the Model Cities program
itself, which was characterized by bitterness and frustration.[23]

More substantial was the organization's work for the Community Analysis Bureau (CAB), whose mission was to operate
the city's Community Renewal Program. LATS prepared the
study design that set the course of CAB's work. It then provided CAB's initial staff until permanent employees could be
hired and trained (by LATS). Thereafter, LATS supplied modest technical assistance and backup. Under this tutelage, CAB
succeeded in producing an impressive body of economic and
demographic data on Los Angeles and developed computerized
data files which may prove useful to future city planning. But
while technically impressive, CAB's data were not organized to
answer any question a Los Angeles policy maker wanted to ask.
Inevitably regarded as a rival by both the city's planning department and its Model Cities program, and lacking a strong
constituency of its own, CAB's opportunity for local influence
and utility lay mainly in providing information the city's political authorities wanted to use. Opting (under LATS guidance)

for technical sophistication instead, it impressed its federal funders—who publicized it as a model—but created only critics in Los Angeles. "I would abolish CAB," commented a city councilman. "It is a means of sapping—of using federal funds we desperately need in other areas for data we don't use."[24]

One of LATS's largest projects was also one of its first. This was the plan for what was originally conceived as a police department command and control communications system. The Watts riots had occurred in 1965. In the following years, through the Law Enforcement Assistance Act, substantial federal monies became available to "modernize" police departments. Working jointly with the Los Angeles Police Department and the aerospace firm TRW, LATS produced a master plan which, beginning from an assessment of police department needs, led to the specification of an integrated "command and control communications data processing system" for all Los Angeles city agencies. As one review of the LATS experience reports, "the report hit the government bureaucracy as a bombshell. . . . The problem was apparently not so much with the style and insensitivity to bureaucratic politics. . . . It was a basic threat to the operations of the various departments."[25] The fire department was expecting to create its own new communications system; so were the police. Other departments were satisfied with existing arrangements, and none wanted to lose control of its own communications. Recognizing that the first report—prepared largely by TRW —was unacceptable, LATS rapidly produced a modified plan reducing somewhat the scope of the proposed system but retaining all emergency services (police, fire, ambulance service, and civil defense) in a single system.

Still wholly characteristic of the "systems" perspectives of the aerospace industry, the plan made great sense technically but deferred only marginally to political realities. The second report, like the first, set off powerful bureaucratic counterpressure for separate communications systems. LATS evidently believed it could offset that pressure by bringing to bear the prestige of General Curtis LeMay, one of its trustees, in a pivotal public meeting. But as it proved, LeMay was no match for the city's fire chief. Each of the Los Angeles departments went its own way. Applying only an engineering perspective to a problem whose difficulty was bureaucratic, the LATS proposal achieved little but hostility. Such an error was understandable in TRW's case. It was a more puzzling failure for LATS, whose business was to mediate between aerospace and municipal perspectives, adapting each to the other.

As difficult for LATS as defining a useful role and acquiring the competence to perform it was the problem of determining who its clients were. LATS had begun as an initiative of the city's business community and then was adopted by Mayor Yorty as an instrument of his own. But as the mayor paid increasing attention to national affairs, his influence in municipal matters—already limited by the vesting of major administrative powers in county agencies and special purpose districts—further declined and that of the city council increased. The council felt no allegiance to LATS. The result was that, having received a $175,000 city contribution in 1970, LATS failed to win council approval for even the $75,000 it sought in 1971 and received no city support thereafter. It then began to depend increasingly on federal monies and to orient itself toward Washington. As a Ford Foundation evaluation concluded:

> LATS evolved from a public-oriented agency, formally tied to the three centers of power in the city government; to an independent agency of the private sector, tied informally to the mayor; to a consulting operation tied to everyone and to no one in the city; to a research institution tied to national research foundations and playing a subordinate role in its remaining activities with the city . . . the simplest evaluation of the performance of LATS is that it has accomplished little or nothing to improve local government in Los Angeles

by application of aerospace technology, by introducing systems analysis, or indeed in any measurable way at all.[26]

By 1974, LATS had stopped work and gone out of existence.

A PARTIAL SUMMING UP

Where do these accounts leave us? Most obviously they suggest that professional consulting organizations of widely different characteristics all met difficulty working for city governments, succeeding perhaps no more often than the universities did. In some cases, the work was conceptually weak; in many more its otherwise sensible conclusions proved infeasible. In either event, it failed to effect results. In almost no case did it lead to a continuing relationship; in some it ended with the collapse of the consulting organization.

Two truths about this pattern are striking. The first is that CONSAD, ADL, McKinsey, RAND, and LATS were not institutions whose staffs sought principally the respect of academic peers rather than the approval of clients. They were not subject to rapid shifts in interest, not committed to solo rather than collaborate work. They were not—at least not to the same degree as academics—concerned with original rather than reliable proposals, or unfamiliar with the perspectives of clients, or unwilling to consider the "external" as well as the "internal" logic of a policy problem. They did not, in short, closely resemble universities. So the traditional explanations of the difficulties encountered by university-based attempts to advise city governments do not seem to explain these failures.

The second truth is that while these organizations encountered such difficulty in working for city governments, they were simultaneously providing more valued and evidently more useful services to other clients. CONSAD is a talented and competent firm. Arthur D. Little and McKinsey & Company are giants in their fields, consulted on matters of importance by thousands of public and corporate clients in the United States and abroad. RAND is one of the nation's premier nonprofit policy research organizations, employed and respected by a broad range of federal clients.

One implication of these histories, then, is that city governments may be peculiarly difficult clients. Their unfamiliarity with large-scale advising relationships; their difficulty in specifying the conditions useful advice must meet; their inability to monitor and participate in the work of advisers; their incapacity to put advice into effect; the political hostility the mere presence of advisers may generate—these characteristics of city government and politics may be the main sources of the difficulties experienced by urban advisers. And if so, then they are the conditions that must be changed or accommodated if advice is to be made more useful.

But if the difficulty is really the nature of the client, then other kinds of evidence should point the same way. It should follow, for example, that university-based research and analysis for other classes of clients should prove more successful than similar service to city governments. Though the evidence is only fragmentary, it suggests exactly that.

Universities' Other Clients

Both as institutions and as aggregations of skilled individuals, universities provide advice to almost the whole spectrum of American institutions. Graduate schools are the most common source of valued expertise, and of these, probably the business schools are called upon most routinely. A 1969 survey of 2,500 business school faculty members found that some 40 percent were paid consultants to private firms.[27] But most schools of engineering have long maintained consulting relationships with the research and production divisions of manufacturing industries, and medical school faculty have traditionally served as consulting physicians. A 1965 survey of University of California faculty members found that roughly 30 percent had performed some consulting activities during the prior year, and the highest percentages of consulting were reported by members of the medical, engineering, and social science faculties.[28]

Specialized schools serving well-defined segments of business or industry—the Colorado School of Mines, for example —have typically maintained particularly close research and consulting relationships with their counterpart industries. As one of the few students of this subject has noted:

As organized industrial research grew in the first decades of the twentieth century, industry interest in university research grew apace. By the 1940's the use of university faculty as consultants, industry support of specific university research projects and graduate fellowships, and some sharing of specialized research equipment had become traditional modes of industry-university interaction.[29]

Relations between universities and the industrial world have probably been closest in the high technology fields and most intense and productive during the 1950s and 1960s. In those years a number of high technology firms were founded expressly to exploit commercial applications of academic research, and their locations (especially surrounding the Massachusetts Institute of Technology and Harvard, and in industrial parks near Stanford University) reflected their continuing symbiosis with university-based talent. There are simply no counterparts in the relations of universities and city governments to linkages as close, continuing, and productive as these.

Though some research conducted for business (especially in the physical sciences) is "basic" or exploratory in character and therefore beyond the scope of any readily imaginable work for urban officials, some very substantial proportion (especially of the studies conducted by engineering, medicine, and business faculty) is by any definition "applied." The ability of universities to provide useful applied work to the corporate world may result in part from the greater relevance to industry and the professions of standard academic skills. But it is also plausible that the greater freedom of private clients to act on the basis of advice should make them regard advice as more valuable. And major commercial clients, by and large, have greater capacity to pose well-specified questions and to understand the answers. It is suggestive that, among corporations, the wealthiest and most sophisticated firms utilize university-based research most intensively. Relationships with consultants are closest and most productive among corporations with substantial technical competence of their own.[30]

The evidence concerning university-based research and consulting for governmental clients other than cities is even thinner than that available on relations with business, but it supports the inference that work for federal and state officials has been both more common and more successful than that for municipal governments.

A 1974 survey of the use of social science by high policy-making officials in a representative group of federal agencies, for example, found that 85 percent of the officials responding "subscribed to the belief that social science knowledge can contribute to the improvement of government policies; 87 percent agreed that the government should make the fullest possible use of social science information. . . ."[31] This high potential demand for social research is matched by a federal ability to fund it. In fiscal 1976 the federal government spent some $1.8 billion to collect social statistics, carry out social research and development, mount various demonstrations, evaluate social programs and policies, and disseminate information about those activities.[32] The level of demand for social research that both those attitudes and those expenditures re-

flect is vastly greater than any counterpart on the municipal
level. How much of such federal expenditures go to universities
is unknown, but the fraction is substantial. A Government
Accounting Office survey of federally-funded program evaluations, for example, shows that while half of the roughly $90
million spent on contract research went to profit-making organizations and 30 percent to nonprofit research firms, 20
percent went to universities.[33]

Even state governments appear to be more frequent and
better-served clients of university-based research than cities.
Though the pattern varies by region and state, the records of
many universities in providing advice to agencies of their state
governments is long and distinguished. This is especially true
in the Southeast and in the Great Lakes region, where the
Universities of North Carolina and of Wisconsin are the best
known but by no means the only examples. In a 1973 survey
of a broad sample of state officials in fourteen southern states,
two-thirds of the officials reported that they "occasionally"
received assistance from local colleges or universities, and 27
percent reported using them "often." And 88 percent of the
officials declared themselves either "satisfied" or "very satisfied" with the last university-based service they had received.[34] These are far higher rates of use and of satisfaction
than those reported by city officials in the partially comparable
study cited in chapter 2.

If state and federal administrators are more common and
more satisfied clients of advice than city officials, it is almost
certainly for several reasons. One is that the composition of
advice to state and federal levels differs from that to cities. We
have noted that advice can be simply descriptive, or can propose a course of action, or detail the steps to implementation.
And we have suggested that the tests for the success of advice
must vary with its intent; the requirement for advice that
describes is simply that the description be accurate. And

though no hard data on the point are available, advice to state and federal agencies is almost certainly more often descriptive than that offered to urban officials. State and federal officials commission attitude surveys, demographic analyses, economic projections, controlled social experiments, program evaluations, and analyses of the sources of social problems: crime, pornography, violence, and the like. Such descriptive studies are not difficult to perform adequately. They typically employ accepted (if imperfect) analytic techniques, moreover, in whose use academic social scientists are commonly expert. And they rarely engender the intensity of resistance encountered by proposals for changes. Yet such studies are rarely performed for urban officials, dominated as they are by more operational concerns and constrained by budgets not intended to support research.

The greater prevalence of descriptive advice to state and local officials should therefore explain some difference in the success rates of advice to them as against advice to urban clients. And it does so without confirming our proposition about the relative weakness of urban consumers of advice. But the other reasons why advice to nonurban officials seems more common and more successful do tend to confirm the proposition. The reasons are related—to each other and to the point just made.

The functions of state and federal government are quite different from those of a municipality. Most city agencies run routine daily operations. They collect garbage, police the streets, put out fires. Most state and federal agencies, on the other hand, set broad policy or allocate funds—for economic development, environmental protection, the alleviation of poverty, and the regulation of business. From that difference many consequences flow. The time-horizons of state and federal agencies tend to be longer and their crises less frequent than those of municipal bureaucracies. They therefore have more time and energy (and funds) for the care and feeding of researchers. They tend to employ persons (and frequently substantial staffs) with training or experience in analytic skills. City officials, on the other hand, typically have not only less need for analysis, but little experience or competence in managing it, no budget to support it, and few employees whom analysts (especially academics) can regard as colleagues. As one academic with experience in city government has remarked, "In a city government, research has to be carried on sub rosa. It's suspect, and no one knows how to use it."[35]

And even where policy-relevant studies of good quality are produced for a municipal client that does know how to use them, the problem of effecting the proposed changes remains. Municipal government, in Frederick O'R. Hayes's phrase, is a "low-change system." Innovation in city agencies must negotiate an obstacle course of civil service regulations, line-item budgets, collective bargaining requirements, community sensitivities, an attentive press, and the charges of a political opposition. A local government agency, in short, is deeply embedded in a local social setting and tightly constrained by it.

Inducers of Change

The hypothesis that city governments are weak and constrained consumers of research draws further support from another body of evidence: the behavior of those nongovernmental institutions which, though they vary greatly on a number of dimensions, have in common a distinctive purpose—not to provide advice but to produce useful change in local government. We glance briefly here at three such institutions: Public Technology, Inc., The Vera Institute of Justice, and the Economic Development Council of New York City.

PUBLIC TECHNOLOGY, INC.

PTI, referred to briefly in chapter 2, is a nonprofit public interest organization, established in 1971 at the initiative of the International City Management Association and intended to speed the application of new technologies to the operations of municipal departments. It solicits from its subscribing local government members statements of the technical problems to which they would most welcome solutions. As to problems which concern a number of jurisdictions, PTI convenes so-called User Requirements Committees. Made up of local administrators, purchasing agents, and union representatives, the committees specify the performance, cost, and availability requirements the new technology should meet. PTI then conducts a search for an appropriate existing product or seeks to stimulate the development of a new one. Once a suitable service or product is found, PTI publicizes it, packages it attractively, and works to get a number of jurisdictions simultaneously to adopt it. Finally, through a staff whose technological and formal analytic capacities are routine but whose interpersonal skills are high, PTI provides some assistance in its trial, adaptation, and initial use. In this way PTI confers not only technical guidance but political insulation. If a project succeeds, the city manager or fire chief or sewage commissioner is encouraged to take the credit. If the project falters, PTI (within limits) accepts the blame and helps try to eliminate the bugs.

This approach to innovation has its drawbacks. Local officials tend to be interested in the innovations most appealing to their bureaucracies or most impressive to their electorates rather than those which, if successful, might make the largest difference. As a result, PTI has invested its greatest effort in developing products like self-contained breathing devices for

fire fighters, underground pipe and conduit locators, portable
traffic counters, and better street-patching material, none of
which are likely to resolve any problem of great scale. But the
process also has powerful advantages. It demonstrates to local
administrators that PTI's purpose is to meet their needs
rather than to broker the new gadgets of private industry. It
attempts to bring city officials into the innovation process at
the beginning, so that they feel the new products or procedures to be *theirs* rather than those of some external force.
And, while aggregating a market for new products, it also
helps insure that localities attempting to use the new technologies will have company; they need not run the political
risks of innovation alone. And, by and large, it works. Better
breathing and fire-finding devices, improved patching material (after some initial failures), fairly sophisticated analytic
techniques for determining appropriate locations for new fire
stations, among other advances, are now effectively in use in
jurisdictions which, without PTI, would not now possess
them.

PTI devotes some attention to stimulating the development
of useful new devices. But its sponsorship, staffing, and method
of operation were each designed not to insure the enlargement
of the *supply* of new technology, but to develop an effective
demand for it. By inducing the early involvement of local
officials, by offering the protection of numbers, by assuring
reliability, and by accepting some responsibility for failure, PTI
has made the trial of innovation safer, easier, and more attractive to local officials.*

An even clearer example of the same strategy at work is
presented by the Vera Institute of Justice.

---

*Not surprisingly, PTI itself has not found the going easy. High costs, management
lapses, and the belief of some subscribers that it should have paid even more attention
to the problems of adapting technology to their own situations have led to wholesale
changes in PTI's management and board, but not to its method of operation.

VERA INSTITUTE OF JUSTICE

Vera began in 1960 when Louis Schweitzer, a prosperous elderly businessman, encountered the fact that New York jails were crowded with persons not convicted of anything. Denied bail or unable to provide it, they were simply awaiting trial— often for months. Schweitzer asked Herbert Sturz, a thirty-year-old acquaintance who was then an editor of *Boy's Life* magazine, to help him see what might be done. Vera has since become a multinational conglomerate of municipal innovation, guided by a prestigious board, widely honored, and solidly supported by foundations, state and local agencies, and foreign governments. But in exploring what could be done for prisoners unable to make bail in Manhattan, Schweitzer and Sturz established the distinctive method that marks Vera's work still.

Interviews with prisoners, lawyers, bondsmen, prosecutors, and judges made it clear that a substantial proportion of those jailed for inability to post bond would have been "good bets" to appear for trial even if they had been set free. Further discussions suggested that the characteristics of accused persons that made them likely to appear voluntarily for trial could be specified with some confidence. These were strong family ties, stable residence, current or recent employment, and absence of prior convictions. It occurred to Schweitzer and Sturz that since bail was intended only to assure appearance at trial, persons exhibiting these characteristics should be released on their recognizance whether they could afford bail or not. That observation was hardly original; nor was it unfamiliar to judges. The question was how to induce the judicial system to act on it.

The answer had to be assembled bit by bit. Patient discussions with Manhattan judges created tolerance for an experiment. Schweitzer's acquaintanceship with Robert Wagner produced the mayor's approval. Schweitzer's own funds and the tempered idealism of a small group of law students recruited by Sturz produced the staff work. The experiment was straightforward. Sturz's staff interviewed all those accused in Manhattan of crimes other than the most serious and assessed their likelihood to appear at trial. When the estimate was favorable, they recommended pretrial release to the judges. The judges made their own decisions. But as the experiment progressed, the staff judgments grew in confidence and accuracy, and the willingness of judges to rely on them expanded accordingly. During the three years of the initial experiment, fewer than 2 percent of those released on staff recommendations failed to appear for trial—a smaller percentage than that of persons who forfeited bail by failing to appear. Analysis of the subsequent trials showed that the project kept out of jail before trial more than 2,000 persons who were later found either not guilty or not appropriate to punish by confinement.

It is worth noting that Sturz and his staff were not neutral observers of these "experiments." They sought a particular result and worked hard to get it. As a Ford Foundation report noted, ". . . when a released defendant had a date for a court appearance, Vera staffers notified him the day before; if he failed to show up, they contacted him again, and if a telephone call was not persuasive, they brought him to court in a taxi."[36] And the result being sought was not simply a successful experiment. It was permanent change in the operation of Manhattan courts, followed by the use of the Manhattan experience as a model elsewhere.

The goal was achieved. The New York Department of Probation now similarly evaluates prisoners for pretrial release in all New York City courts. The Manhattan bail project stimu-

lated similar bail reform initiatives throughout the United
States and was largely responsible for the passage of federal bail
reform legislation. A simple, single idea was made to work by
a potent combination: a concern for results; a slow, persistent,
non-threatening approach; the cultivation of support at several
levels; the use of a well-designed "experiment" to induce reform; and the capacity to bear the costs—in funds, initiative,
managerial effort, and potential blame—of the experiment.

Early in the bail experiment, Schweitzer and Sturz formally
established the Vera Institute of Justice as a base for their
work. Vera's second project illustrates another source of its
strength. It began, again, with a well-understood problem and
an obvious but risky solution. The problem was that except for
traffic and minor regulatory offenses, all arrests in New York
City set off a sequence of events which dislocated the life of
the accused, wasted an enormous number of police man-hours,
and burdened the criminal justice system. The arresting officer
took the accused to a police station for "booking," and then
to court (if it was open) for arraignment or to jail overnight if
court hours had ended. Depending on the time of day, the
process might take from six to eighteen hours. If unable to post
bail, the accused might end that period back in jail. The arresting officer, accompanying the accused from scene of crime to
station house to court, was unavailable for patrol duties. If the
arrest occurred toward the end of the officer's tour, the process
meant that he would be hours late getting home—hours for
which he would be only partially compensated. Some observers
of the New York City Police Department believed those circumstances created a strong disincentive to arrest toward the
end of tours.

The solution Vera proposed in 1964, for a limited number
of crimes and for accused persons who appeared responsible,
was to issue simple summonses following arrest, as in traffic

offenses. The police commissioner rejected the idea. Vera countered by bringing pressure on him from an important judge and by preparing to try the idea with a suburban police department. The commissioner reluctantly agreed to a trial in one precinct. Again Vera provided funds, staff, and management. Again it began conservatively, selecting persons with strong neighborhood attachments accused of relatively minor offenses to recommend for release to summonses. Again the experiment was broadened in scope and institutionalized after proving successful. Indeed, shortly after the favorable preliminary results were in, Sturz appears to have suggested to the organizers of a national conference on criminal justice that the commissioner be asked to speak, and then to have prepared for the commissioner a talk on police innovation in New York City in which he could claim credit for the early success of the summons experiment.

The year before the project began, a total of sixty-seven summonses were issued in New York City for nontraffic offenses. In 1971, three years after the new procedure had been adopted throughout the city, more than 32,000 summonses were issued. Strikingly, all the affected parties regarded themselves as better off. Accused persons avoided indignity and lost time. The Budget Bureau estimated savings in police and court man-hours at some $5 million annually. Police officers welcomed the reduction in paperwork and involuntary overtime. The commissioner enjoyed his reputation as a successful innovator.

Vera has since cultivated strong relationships with police, judicial, and correctional officials at state and federal levels and has developed successful "experiments" in sentencing, in the treatment of alcoholics and drug addicts, and in the rehabilitation of convicts. It has spawned associated institutions in a variety of U.S. cities and in several abroad. But its approach remains unchanged. It offers not novelty of concept but assistance in execution, insulation against risks, and good odds on winning a prize more valuable than any other to public officials: public approval. "They are not a fault-finding organization," remarked a former New York City police commissioner laconically. The director of Vera's Cincinnati offshoot put it more directly: "We're in the credit business," he remarked, and added, "And you've got to be sure there's credit to give. Design the experiment so it works on day one, not on day ninety. You may never get to day ninety."[37]

THE ECONOMIC DEVELOPMENT COUNCIL*

The record of New York City's Economic Development Council (EDC) is interesting because the council's work with the city's government has produced failures and mixed results as well as successes, and because the reasons for those differing results seem clear.

EDC was founded in 1965. It represented an attempt by executives of a number of large New York City-based banks, insurance firms, oil companies, and major industrial organizations to reverse the decline in the city's economy then becoming apparent. In its first years the council focused on creating new private sector jobs in the city and on pressing for reorganization of the whole structure of municipal government through a proposed "Little Hoover Commission." Neither effort took hold. In 1968, under the leadership of George Champion, a former chairman of the board of the Chase Manhattan Bank, EDC adopted a new strategy. It concluded that municipal services must be improved one at a time and that its own comparative advantage lay in speeding that improvement by lending to city agencies managerial and operational talent

*This account is based largely on David Rogers's analysis in *Can Business Management Save the Cities?* (New York: The Free Press, 1978).

drawn from the business community. EDC would become the senior consultant to city departments; experienced, dedicated, and free of charge.

EDC then undertook a substantial consulting relationship with the city's court system. It persisted in that work, stuck to problems of management and procedure where its expertise gave it leverage, benefited from the appointment of an administrative judge eager to induce change, and helped bring about a number of useful reforms. But the municipal function EDC came to regard as most important to improve was education. Many of its most influential members believed that better schools were essential both to retaining New York City's middle class and to training a productive labor force. So, over the following six years, in a series of projects EDC devoted money, talent, and substantial attention to the city's schools. The results were mixed.

EDC's first school project reflected two assumptions. Both were natural to corporate officers, both had motivated its previous attempt at city-wide government reorganization, and both were mistaken. EDC supposed that control was exerted downward from the top of public organizations; and that arrangements obviously more "rational" or "efficient" would readily win acceptance.

The project was begun in 1971 at the invitation of the new chancellor of the city's schools. It involved rethinking the management structure of the Board of Education to improve efficiency and to facilitate the new patterns of decentralized school decision making then emerging. EDC's recommendations were prepared and submitted in six months. They called mainly for the creation of four new deputy chancellors, each intended to provide high-level attention, to major curricular and administrative issues.

The board deferred considering the plan for fourteen months, then imposed changes EDC regarded as unreasonable, and finally approved it only after EDC's threat to provide no further assistance unless action was taken. The assistance EDC most wanted to provide was help in recruiting qualified officials to fill the new posts, as well as the positions of chancellor and deputy chancellor, which were then vacant. Authorized to do so by the board, EDC conducted a nationwide search. It submitted to the board a list of distinguished candidates, almost all unknown in New York City and chosen wholly on professional qualifications. Ignoring the list, the board then chose, from persons known to it, two Jews, two blacks, an Italian, a Puerto Rican, and an Irishman. "[EDC was] really naive about the politics of education, and you can't separate the management of education from its politics,"[38] remarked a board member. The experience diminished EDC's naiveté. It did not again attempt to impose a technocratic solution upon a political problem. It began instead to address operational problems at the school and district level.

One such effort involved the Bureau of Supplies, the unit which purchased, stored, and distributed all materials used in the schools. Its deficiencies were wholly characteristic of a weakly managed public sector support function. The bureau's orders from producers bore no relation to usage rates (its inventory contained a 474-year supply of one item); it neither sought nor received volume discounts; it delivered needed items to a school only after the orders from a single borough were sufficient to fill a truck, and its physical layout was chaotic. The bureau's problems, therefore, were not hard to identify. Indeed, they had been fully specified by previous consultants, who had also proposed suitable reforms. EDC helped the bureau because it offered not a proposed solution but working-level leadership in accomplishing it.

The warehouse specialist that EDC loaned the bureau was a man of modest background who had worked his way up in the supply arm of Continental Can Company. Though originally expected by EDC to perform a study, he seized the chance to accomplish change rather than to recommend it. He encouraged and taught bureau staff to lay out a physical plan for their new warehouse so that most commonly ordered items were most accessible. He showed how usage data for supplies could be readily compiled and how purchasing could be varied to correspond with usage. To help design a computerized information system he borrowed two additional technicians through EDC. And his encouragement persuaded the bureau to increase the number of deliveries to schools, which not only improved service but reduced inventory costs.

The project was a complete success, providing more responsive service to schools, lowering costs, and improving bureau morale. As David Rogers has pointed out, the problems here were technical and managerial, not political, and the capacities EDC could bring to bear were appropriate ones. And, largely by accident, the EDC staffer assigned to the task was particularly well suited to it. As Rogers has noted:

The irony of his consulting contribution was that he found it very difficult to write up his final report, which, while interesting, communicated only the bare outlines of what he had contributed or of the dynamics of the process. For the Bureau this was of no importance, since he had already made many of his contributions long before the report was written. As one of them commented at the end: "You know, John came to work without a briefcase. He looked around, rolled up his sleeves, asked if he could see how the warehouse operated and what might be done to improve it. We didn't need any more briefcase guys with fancy reports!"[39]

As it learned its way into the New York City School system, EDC was able to help with less mechanical problems. Probably the clearest example of such assistance was EDC's work with the George Washington High School.

In 1970, George Washington represented the "blackboard

jungle" at its wildest. Previously one of the city's premier academic high schools, it had admirably served striving children of the middle class and had graduated Jacob Javits, Arthur Miller, Henry Kissinger, and Kenneth Clark, among other luminaries. But by the late 1960s, the school's feeder neighborhoods had experienced waves of ethnic succession. The student body was three-fourths black or Spanish-speaking and almost entirely poor. Many of the teachers, strongly backed by their union, were determined to preserve traditional standards and practices, but when EDC representatives first visited the school:

> . . . police were stationed throughout the halls . . . barricades were prominently in evidence. Four principals had served . . . during the previous year . . . parents were divided into militant factions . . . disaffected students whiled away most of the days in the cafeteria; neighborhood merchants closed their stores when George Washington's students left in the afternoon; and the threat and reality of violence against any person, young or adult, pervaded the campus.[40]

With assistance from The Institute for Educational Development (IED), an educational consulting firm, EDC began by convening teachers, the acting principal, students, and—after some skillful diplomacy—a hostile parents' group. It got them jointly to identify the most critical problems and plan an agenda for change. That accomplished, EDC and IED staffers, trained in organizational development techniques, served in two capacities. They mediated disputes among the participants, establishing an office in the school which became a focal point for complaints, suggestions, and the resolution of conflicts. And they brought outside resources to bear on problems the planning group had given priority. A General Motors commissary executive was brought in to recommend changes in the school's cafeteria. A bank officer designed improvements in security arrangements. EDC paid for the initial costs of an intensive remedial program that sharply raised the percentage of passing grades among its participants. Business and professional contacts were exploited to stimulate students to consider vocational possibilities. And an athletic program was designed to absorb excess energies and create the beginnings of school spirit.

George Washington remained a troubled school. But by helping its factions find common objectives and then advancing those objectives by drawing on its own funds and business skills, EDC helped turn the school away from chaos and collapse.

COMMON TRAITS

Disparate as they are, PTI, Vera, and EDC share revealing traits. Each is well-grounded politically. Each operates only in an arena where it has a comparative advantage; none holds itself out as a general-purpose adviser. Each has access to funds beyond those its local government clients can supply. Each seeks not to provide advice but to induce change. Though to varying degrees, each has been successful in inducing change. And—most striking from the perspective of this study—each sees the leverage for change not in the generation of new proposals but in assisting local governments to test and adopt reforms or innovations that are rarely complex or original. And each accomplishes that by focusing on the concerns of city officials and of the bureaucracies they direct. Each finds ways of reducing the financial costs, minimizing the political risks, and limiting the managerial effort required to test the innovations and to make them operational. Each, in short, understands that augmenting the capacity of local government to act on good advice is far more valuable (and more rare) than providing the advice.

Capable Consumers

The last of the phenomena which appear to show that the tightest constraints on useful advice to city governments arise not from shortcomings in particular sources of expertise but from the nature of local government is the performance of those rare city officials who are adept at stimulating and using advice. Though, again, the available evidence is far from comprehensive, it is virtually uniform: such officials are able to draw useful advice from all sources, including universities.

We have already touched upon at least three examples. As noted in chapter 2, innovation-minded operating-level officials in several departments of the city of Cincinnati have been able routinely to draw upon interested and knowledgeable faculty members of the University of Cincinnati, even though formal programs of university-city cooperation broke down. Similarly, the Environmental Protection Administration of New York City, determined to reform garbage collection procedures and able, by use of its own analytic staff, to commission, understand, and help apply research, profited not only from the services of McKinsey & Company but also from the work of the analysts from the State University of New York at Stony Brook. Again, as described in chapter 4, an assistant administrator of New York City's Housing and Development Administration, who was experienced in designing and monitoring policy-relevant research, was able to meld the efforts of RAND, McKinsey, and a research group at Rutgers University headed by Professor George Sternlieb into a well-focused and—as it turned out—highly influential research program.

Indeed, it appears that a high proportion of innovation-minded mayors, city managers, department heads, and bureau chiefs have reached out to universities (among other sources of information and proposals) and that they have succeeded more often than they have failed in using the resulting university contributions. Mayor Lee of New Haven, for example, one of the most successful and innovative American mayors of the early 1960s, leaned heavily on Yale University—and especially on its law school—for advice on a wide range of substantive issues, assistance in recruiting, and exploiting useful contacts in the federal government. His relationship with the school, wholly informal, was close and productive. William Donaldson, perhaps the most outstanding example of an innovative city manager in the late 1960s and early 1970s, was able during his tenure in Tacoma, Washington to draw useful advice and expertise with apparently equal ease from the Boeing Corporation, the Battelle Institute, the RAND Corporation, various local business firms, the University of Washington, and universities farther afield. Donaldson went so far as to create a position of "economist in residence" in city hall, and the first incumbent of that position, a well-chosen professor from Penn State, proved helpful almost from the start.

The truth, in short, appears to be—as Dr. Ralph Thayer, director of the Urban Studies Institute of the University of New Orleans, has put it—that "Where cities work well, universities can work well *with* them."[41]

CHAPTER 5

What Have We Learned?

When Yen Ho was about to take up his duties as
tutor to the heir of Ling, Duke of Wei, he went to
Ch'u Po Yu for advice. "I have to deal," he said,
"with a man of depraved and murderous disposi-
tion. . . . How is one to deal with a man of this
sort?" "I am glad," said Ch'u Po Yu, "that you
asked this question. . . . The first thing you must
do is not to improve him, but to improve your-
self."

TAOIST STORY, quoted by Arthur Waley in
Three Ways of Thought in Ancient China.

We now have before us a considerable body of evidence. What
does it show? This chapter attempts to identify a number of
lessons and to group them in terms of their applicability: to
producers of advice for local government (academic and otherwise); to consumers of such advice (principally officials of local
government); and to interested third parties (mainly foundations and state and federal agencies).

Some General Truths

At least four simple rules apply to all advice, whether intended to propose, to implement, or merely to inform.

First, there must be a client—a local agency responsible for the subject being investigated. Obvious as the point is, once stated, it is sometimes overlooked. Where the condition is not met (as in RAND's first Human Resources work in New York, and in the Pittsburgh and San Francisco CRP's cases), no advice can be useful because no agency has the interest or responsibility to use it. The second condition is simply that there be a specified problem or issue, or a number of them. Where an adviser is set loose simply to "do good," his advice (as the Tulsa case and most of the urban observatory experience demonstrate) is more likely to produce net detriment than benefit. It will distract, annoy, or agitate more often than it assists. The third condition is that the purported adviser have a genuine and relevant expertise. Purported expertise may be spurious (as was true in virtually all cases where the adviser's promise was to analyze a city in "holistic" terms) or irrelevant to the problem at hand. Finally, adviser and client must communicate. The client must be able to assess the probable utility of the adviser's conclusions; the adviser must be able to convey his results in terms the client can understand.*

When a problem is small in scale, technical in nature, and within the responsibility of a single municipal department, city governments can often meet their share of these conditions.

---

*This may mean orally rather than in writing, and sooner and more briefly than an adviser (especially an academic) finds comfortable. This may hold true even where the client is represented by a former academic. An aide to Boston's Mayor Kevin White has remarked, "I'm an academic by background, but my hostility to academics grew fast when I took this job. They came and proposed studies, went away a long time, and then produced something very long. No one read it. Even I didn't read it. I now do business face to face and on the phone. I don't read *anything* long."[1]

They are likely then to be willing clients, able to specify their needs and to assess the work done for them. The modeling of Jamaica Bay and the revisions in New York City's Sanitation work schedules are good examples. Correspondingly, where the issue is small in scale and within the competence of a single academic discipline, a university (or individual academics) can often meet the conditions set for providers of advice.

Where the purpose of the work is not simply to inform, but to propose change or assist in its accomplishment, then a number of additional conditions must be met. Probably most important, the client agency must have some incentive to effect change. The incentive may arise from its own professional standards, from a mayor's pressure, or from public demands; whatever the source, it must make some substantial fraction of the agency hospitable to change. Secondly, the proposals offered by the adviser must be broadly consistent with the client's values. They cannot affront the client's self-esteem or threaten its independence—as LATS's proposals threatened the Los Angeles Fire Department, for example. Recommendations may safely affront the values of some small fraction of a client agency, but not its political officials or dominant elements of its bureaucracy.

If the client were a corporation run on strict hierarchical lines, probably no further conditions would need to be met. The problem being real, the advice informed and relevant, the proposals not inherently offensive, and those in authority having an incentive to act, action would follow and change would result. But if the foregoing chapters have shown anything, it is that city governments are not simple hierarchical systems run on authoritarian lines. They are complex, open systems serving diverse and partially contradictory goals, responding to conflicting constituencies, whose authority is diffused, whose inertia is enormous, and whose ability to plan and direct substantial change is excruciatingly small.

This being true, large additional burdens fall on any provider of advice who intends to actually affect events. Like the small RAND staff in the fire dispatching story, the adviser may have to persistently explain and defend his proposal, and to modify it to meet objections. Like the Stony Brook staff member implanted for a year at a sanitation district headquarters, he may need to unravel patiently the most trivial problems of implementation and see the proposal through to a test. And, like Vera or EDC, the adviser must be prepared to provide his own managerial talent to insure that when the proposal is first tried, the will, interest, and capacity to make it work are present. Finally, the adviser may be required to bring the dowry of his own funding to the relationship so that such intensive care does not prove impossibly expensive to the patient.

I have written elsewhere that

. . . even where the right problem (or one of the right problems) is being addressed, the engineer, the operations researcher, the statistician, the economist are very likely to want to address it only in terms of their professional skills, and then to stop. The researcher performs his regressions or builds his simulation; he identifies an apparent solution. He presents it as lucidly and persuasively as he can to his client. And at that point he believes his job is done. His training tells him he has reached the limits of his professional competence. His stomach tells him the rest is politics, which is dangerous, or management, which is dull. He wants no further responsibility, and he may be offered none. . . . The analyst wants to function simply as an analyst; that is the only function in which he imagines he has a comparative advantage.

But is it? If he has examined even casually the system that must receive recommendations, understand them, explain them, dampen fears about them, pay for them, modify them, try them, and live with their consequences, good and ill, then he must notice that this system is poorly developed in cities; weak, immature, and vulnerable. And it is weakest where the problem is not "where should we be going?" but "how do we get there—or somewhere near there—from here?" Ends and means interact. And to the degree they are separable,

means pose the harder challenge. For both reasons, those who propose ends, and who care about outcomes, must care about means.[2]

But the point here is larger. The adviser must not merely
care about means and assist with means; he may have to take
principal responsibility for inventing, testing, refining, and paying for means. In the classical model of advice relationships—
the conception most people carry in their heads—the adviser
analyzes a problem, reaches a conclusion, presents that conclusion to a decision maker, and then withdraws. The decision
maker then decides or fails to decide; the responsibility, in any
event, has shifted to him. What we have found is that where
the receiver of advice is a unit of local government, that model,
much of the time, is worse than useless; it is deceptive. It
conceals the fact that in the realm of urban innovation, the
adviser who intends to help must compensate for the deficiencies of the advised—providing the funds for tests or experiments the city agency cannot pay for; substituting his own
self-discipline for the client's incapacity to monitor his work;
and providing the political protection and managerial support
this peculiarly vulnerable client may require.

Indeed it is fair to say that in the various histories sketched
in previous chapters, there is no case of innovation achieved on
the basis of external advice except where either the client
agency had the resources to understand and supervise the work
and to put it into effect, or (more commonly) the advising
entity took full responsibility for producing work of quality and
utility, and for introducing or helping introduce the proposed
changes itself.

Conversely, every failure of proposed change we have seen
has involved both a less capable or less interested client and an
adviser unwilling or unable to provide such "intensive care."
And in every case where these failures have achieved a considerable scale, the relationship between adviser and city client

has been funded by some third party. The Pittsburgh and San Francisco CRP cases, the Tulsa experience, USAC, and the urban observatories are all in point.

Considerably more detailed and perhaps more operationally useful lessons can be elicited from the histories we have reviewed. They appear most clearly if one focuses separately on three partially overlapping but distinguishable kinds of conclusions: those of greatest interest of producers of advice to city governments; those which most concern government officials themselves, the consumers of advice; and those that apply to third parties seeking to stimulate or to fund relationships between cities and external advisers.

Lessons for Producers

Any attempt to advise "a ruler who is not wise himself" (or who is only marginally a "ruler") involves special problems and creates special responsibilities. The problems are principally three. First, unless the adviser is dealing with an unusual city agency, he will receive less guidance than he needs. His client is not likely to provide him with anything comparable to the twenty-page analysis that gave clear focus to Stony Brook's work for the New York City Sanitation Department—a detailed statement of the problem; a review of alternative solutions already considered; and an analysis of the political, bureaucratic, and fiscal constraints that would affect the choice of a solution. So the adviser must find some way to provide such guidance for himself—and to do it early.

The second problem is that the adviser will find himself, like it or not, engaged in politics. There are few findings and no recommendations which do not tend to advance the interests of some person or group or to jeopardize the interests of others.

"How odd it is," Charles Darwin remarked, "that anyone should not see that all observation must be for or against some view if it is to be of any service."[3] It is odd, but common, perhaps especially among academics. So the adviser must understand that however technical his advice, however "value free" his method, however innocent his intentions, his work, unless it is trivial, will suggest shifts in power, responsibility, role, or resources. He will be engaged, in short, in politics. It may be the obvious party politics of metropolitan elections or the covert bureaucratic politics—no less viciously fought—of intra-agency advantage. But politics it is. The adviser must therefore expect to find his results attacked (and misrepresented), his motives questioned, his costs scrutinized, his methods derided. He can expect blame if recommendations are tried and fail, and little praise if they work. It is not an assignment to everyone's taste.

The third problem is that, if the advice proposes substantial change, it is a near certainty that the change will not be accomplished unless the adviser himself is prepared to devote months and perhaps years helping to bring it about. Even then it may not even be attempted, and if attempted, it may not be achieved.

The special responsibilities of working for so hobbled a client as a unit of city government may be more burdensome than the problems. It is a standard truth of the commercial management consulting business that there are corporations no consultant can help. Often they are found in highly protected market positions, insulated by natural monopolies or strong patent protection. They are characterized by weak management, little planning or analytic capacity, and low levels of imagination and initiative. Generally, they promote from within, hire only at the bottom, and fire seldom or never. Management may be aware of inefficiency, but it cannot muster the will or energy to change. The underlying reason is that it knows it does not have to; the firm will survive in any event. These are corporations, of course, that greatly resemble public bureaucracies. Virtually all of local government qualifies by these standards as a corporation no consultant can help. Or more accurately, such clients can be helped, but not by advice.* The adviser, as we have now repeatedly argued, must supply whatever resources the client cannot. Where the goal is useful change, there is much to be supplied. If he takes an appropriate view of his job, then, and has the motivation to perform it fully, how should the adviser proceed?

THE LESSONS

The histories we have sketched suggest a number of guidelines for advisers to local government.

Identify the Client. Advice whose purpose is mainly to describe may not need to be designed for use by a particular client. An analysis of demographic or economic trends in a metropolitan area, for example, may have implications for many levels of public and private decision making; its full import may exceed the authority of any of those levels to affect. But advice that proposes some particular action takes responsibility for helping produce a result. That responsibility is poorly discharged unless the advice fits the perceptions, values, and capacities of a specific client—a person or agency with motives to accept the advice and the ability to apply it. Where an operating agency itself has contracted for advice, the identity of the client is unambiguous. In the more common cases in which a foundation or federal department or municipal overhead agency (like New York City's Budget Bureau) is paying

---

*Omitted from consideration here are circumstances in which the municipal client can be helped without itself acting—principally where it can use the adviser's product directly in its relation with another level of government. LATS's preparation of a model city application and Denver's use of the Urban Observatory's findings on who uses the city's public facilities are two examples.

the adviser, the client's identity may be far less obvious. The first task then is to decide who the client is.

Learn from the Client. The adviser needs from a client agency not merely points of contact, but working colleagues. He needs them for many purposes. One is to clarify and perhaps redefine the nature of the problem. A city agency is far more likely to know that something is wrong than to know what is wrong and why. Recall the original focus of New York City's housing officials not on conserving the huge existing supply of rental housing but on building new publicly-assisted units. Redefining the problem required a client to talk to. The adviser also needs advice, as these histories have repeatedly made clear, on the constraints that will determine whether his client can act on his proposals—the political and bureaucratic facts of life that determine what is feasible and under what conditions.

Earn His Trust. Officials of local government are much like other people: they accept advice more readily from persons they know and trust than from those they do not. So if the adviser wishes his advice to have weight, he must give his client a basis for confidence in his values, motives, and judgment. He has entered a professional relationship that requires as much discretion and loyalty to the client as legal or medical relations do. Both parties must be confident that obligation will be met.

Find Internal Champions. The cases illustrate a truth well documented in the literature of organizational innovation: in any large organization (and perhaps especially in local government), officials are far more likely to become champions of change if they regard the proposed innovations as their own rather than those of outsiders. And the more they have participated in the fact-finding, analysis, and shaping of conclusions, the more proprietary their feelings will be.

Find the Right Ones. To the catalog of reasons for developing close working relations with the client should be added a caution. Advisers tend to relate to the persons in the client agency with whom they feel most comfortable. For technically trained analysts, these persons are likely to be members of the agency's planning or analytic staffs, or perhaps young staff assistants to major officials. The temptation to rely mainly on such persons is understandable; they share with the analysts common training, values, and vocabulary, and a common freedom from commitment to things as they are. But planning and analytic staffs are often outsiders in their own agencies. They may have little influence and less sensitivity to the operational difficulties around which innovations must be designed. Young staff assistants add to those shortcomings unstable priorities and erratic career paths. They are not likely to be still in position a year or two afterwards, when the conclusive tests of strength will occur. Moreover, as RAND's experience with the central analytic staff of New York City's Health and Hospitals Administration suggests, internal analysts may ultimately see external advisers as rivals. Having no source of influence themselves except the good opinion of their line supervisors, they may be reluctant to see those superiors develop a good opinion of outsiders whose functions are similar. So the adviser is generally best served by support from cultures different from his own —in particular, line officials, political, or career. He should seek to make them his chief points of contact.

Look for Discontent. In choosing (or accepting) problems to examine, try to work mainly in areas where the client is already convinced that something important is wrong. It is not necessary that the agency understand exactly what is wrong or that it foresee the solution. But at the end of the adviser's work the agency will choose between change and stability. In such a choice inertia normally weighs the odds heavily toward things as they are. But where the agency has already accepted the necessity for change, it will regard its choice as lying between the adviser's recommendation and some other proposal whose

authorship, scope, and motivation cannot be known. In that
choice, the adviser's odds are far better.

Avoid Program Evaluations. Using discontent is productive; attempting to create it is not. Since nothing works as well
as it might, and since evaluators demonstrate their acuteness
most readily by finding fault, program evaluations are almost
always critical. Even when they propose correctives, evaluations focus mainly on fault: questionable policies, probable
inefficiencies, inadequate foresight, perhaps a taint of fraud.
That may be tolerable for a new administrator but not for a
veteran. And in either event it makes enemies of his career
subordinates. (Recall the Cleveland manpower study.) More
important, it serves little purpose. Proposals for change can
document clearly enough, though implicitly, what is wrong.
And their emphasis is far more welcome and more useful: not
what is wrong and who should take the blame, but how service
or policy or operations can be improved.

Produce Something Useful Fast. No matter how prestigious or highly recommended, an adviser new to a client must
establish his credentials. Where the problem being addressed
is relatively simple and the time required is short, the advice
itself may do that. But if the ultimate product is complex and
will take some time to produce, then some useful interim
product should be contrived. The cases where it was not (virtually all the USAC situations, among many examples) are largely
failures. Local government lacks the patience, the resources,
the confidence, and the long-time horizons to support product-
less research or analysis for very long. "Slippery water" and the
Denver Observatory's findings on public facilities' user-pat-
terns suggest, in differing ways, how early helpfulness can sustain a client's confidence that future products are worth waiting for and investing in.

Promise No Breakthroughs. Some agencies of the federal
government, and especially the armed services, are experienced

in contracting for products beyond the current state of an art. Such clients understand that in technically ambitious projects cost overruns, time extensions, and performance shortcomings are normal. The armed services are wealthy enough and (except in time of war) patient enough to accept those consequences. But local governments are in a very different position. With the exception of the mathematical modeling of Jamaica Bay, it is hard to identify a single case in which an attempt to apply complex and untried methods to local government problems succeeded. Certainly the USAC experience, the Pittsburgh and San Francisco CRP's, and the "holistic" systems work in Tulsa were all clear-cut failures. Given several additional years, substantially increased funding (and more responsible management), the USAC and CRP efforts might have yielded useful results. But the adviser to cities cannot count on more time or money, and responsible management alone is not sufficient. He is well advised, therefore, to avoid promising a service or product he does not yet know how to produce.

Unusable Advice Is Not Good Advice. A responsible adviser takes his clients as he finds them. He may conclude that a particularly weak city agency is incapable of improvement, that the problem he is asked to address is intractable, or that his own analytic or political abilities are inadequate to the task. If so, he should decline to help. But if he does agree to help, then help is what he owes. Unless the advice is intended merely to inform, elegant analysis alone does not qualify. Technical ingenuity does not qualify. Good intentions do not qualify. The client is owed the kind of assistance he can use.

To the Client Belongs the Credit. If reform is accomplished and public credit is due, it is the client who should get it. The rule is functional: advisers who absorb what blame they can for failure but forsake praise for success are more welcome and more potent. "You can get a lot done in government" goes the familiar observation, "if you don't care who gets the credit." But the functional reason is reinforced by one of fairness. No matter how adroit, accomplished, or self-disciplined the adviser; no matter how deeply he engages in the details of implementation, his recommendations may not work. Or they may work poorly or produce unforeseen side effects. If so, it will be a public official who will ultimately pay the price. The adviser goes on to other advice, as President Kennedy once observed, but the official goes on to elections. The public holds the official responsible, not his advisers; and it should. If the client must take blame for failure, he is entitled to credit for success.

ACADEMICS AS ADVISERS

In addition to the injunctions that apply to all advisers to city governments, a number appear to apply especially to academics.

Consider Whether You Can Do the Job. Universities as institutions and academics as individuals should be clear about their probable disadvantages as advisers to local government. These are not merely the characteristics recounted in chapter 2—the concern for the good opinion of academic peers rather than that of clients; probable interest in the general principle rather than the particular application; the incentives to produce an original rather than a reliable conclusion, and so forth —though these alone will often disqualify. There are at least two further problems: universities as institutions are poorly structured to ensure that specified products are delivered by particular times, and academics as individuals may be ill-equipped to persuade, support, and provide political cover for distracted, unintellectual, and probably skeptical government clients.

As to the managerial record of universities, recall the urban observatory cases. As to the psychic qualifications of academics, consider the attitude toward city officials of many of the academics involved in the Pittsburgh CRP: as Brewer makes clear, it was one of lightly-disguised contempt. And even where so corrosive an attitude is absent, academic advisers may still be unable to sustain the self-effacing persistence required to induce substantial change in a municipal bureaucracy. Indeed they may find it difficult to maintain even a more straightforward relationship. Professor Stanley Altman, a key figure in Stony Brook's successful work for New York City's Environmental Protection Administration, has said of work for urban clients:

> The psychic highs may be quite high—you get your name in the papers and letters of commendation from politicians. But the frustrations are intense. In the classroom you're a king, and you go into a city office thinking you are there to help and deserve some gratitude or at least respect. But people may not even have the time to talk to you, or they suspect your motives, or they're just rude.[4]

There are certainly differences among the disciplines. Professors of law, medicine, architecture, or of the applied sciences—fields accustomed to clients—are more likely than others to be equipped for such relationships. But professionals in any field who regard themselves primarily as researchers or teachers may find the strain considerable. Reflecting on their own capacities, tolerances, and schedules, academics may conclude that they are ill suited to assist a difficult and perhaps reluctant client with a complex problem.

Consider Why You Want the Job. In the 1960s and early 1970s, "relevance" prompted many academics to consult with urban governments. But notions of relevance are fleeting. City hall may be "where the action is" today, but tomorrow the Congress may have it, or the environmental movement, or the

Pentagon. And today's relevance may tomorrow seem merely
faddish.

The search for fresh sources of funds, clearly, was another
motive. But the past decade demonstrates that neither local
governments nor their federal and foundation patrons are reliable long-term supporters of analysis or advice.

The notion that the city might be a laboratory, a setting for
new and important discovery, was yet another attraction. But
experience suggests that the urban laboratory is a peculiarly
difficult and distracting one, where experiments are uncon-
trolled and uncontrollable, ambient conditions unstable, the
hypotheses to be tested poorly formulated or nonexistent, the
first principles of "urban science" still undiscovered. Experiments in such a laboratory may prove little.

Consider the Costs. Becoming embroiled in local decision
making and hence in local politics may prove costly to a university, particularly to a public university dependent on broad
public support. The danger may arise either from unpopular
conclusions on a sensitive topic (the legitimacy of teenage
behavior in Tulsa) or from sloppy or irrelevant work (the Pittsburgh CRP and Cleveland Observatory).

A higher cost may arise from distortions of purpose. While
serving poorly as public advisers, academics may slight the roles
for which they are better equipped and which comprise their
reason for being: teaching and research. And those more ele-
mental functions have civic virtues of their own: over the long
run they create more knowledgeable citizens, and local officials
more alert to the help that research and analysis might provide.

If You're Going To Do It, Do It Right. For universities,
doing it right involves first two negative injunctions: avoid
grandiose plans and avoid institutional relationships.

Asked how he would stimulate useful assistance from a university, William Donaldson, who succeeded Robert Turner as
the city manager of Cincinnati, responded:

I'd hire a guy and tell him to spend six months wandering around city agencies talking to people about what interested them and what they thought their problems were. Then he'd spend another six months circulating in the university seeing who knew what and who was inclined to be helpful. And I would tell that guy that if he ever held a meeting of more than three people he'd be fired.[5]

The plan may be overly severe, but its principle is sound. As Cincinnati's previous experience suggests, "bridges" officially constructed between a whole city government and a university as an institution usually collapse. I know of none that carried any substantial traffic. Nor is that surprising. Most city governments offer neither an appropriate central point of contact for the university nor any central funding source. And there is no reason for such a centralized relationship. It would be useful only if, by drawing on resources from many schools and departments, the university could offer a mayor or city manager or city council analyses of the city as a systematic whole. But that capacity is nowhere in sight. Pending its development, broad institutional relationships between cities and universities simply bring together uninterested mayors and powerless deans.

As the Donaldson remark suggests, the advising relationships that work best between scholars and officials are those at lower levels. When a deputy fire chief or assistant sewer commissioner or public health district director encounters a specific problem to which the skills of a professor of engineering or business administration or medicine are clearly relevant, and when the official himself selects the professor from whom he wants help and specifies the kind of help required, then—all our evidence shows—the relationship is likely to be productive. Such relationships require from university administrators little but toleration.

You Have Some Comparative Advantage. City governments are rarely adept at searching widely for appropriate advisers. Therefore, especially for less cosmopolitan cities, local academics may be the obvious or only choice. But such a choice may confer some potential advantages. Cities normally cannot afford (or are unwilling to pay) the high overhead costs of professional research and consulting firms. Academics should be able to offer lower costs. The professors of a local university are likely also to enjoy both a prestige that outside consultants may lack and a network of contacts in the city's social and political structure. And universities may themselves be major political forces. For one thing, they are substantial employers. The University of Pittsburgh, including its associated hospitals, meets Pittsburgh's largest payroll. The University of Nebraska is the largest employer in the state. Strong support for innovation from members of such faculties, therefore, may lend the proposal substantial weight.

If You Can't Do It Right, Don't Do It. The final injunction is the sum of the others. If the adviser's purpose is not simply to inform but to help induce useful change, then the numerous and burdensome conditions we have been reviewing must be met. If they cannot, the odds are high against the intended change taking effect. If the client is wise he will not seek advice under those circumstances. If the client is not wise, the prospective adviser must be wise on his behalf: he must decline the assignment. It seems reasonable to expect that academics, for whom consulting is not the sole source of income, should observe the rule more faithfully than professional consultants and researchers.

Lessons for Consumers

Many of the lessons the cases teach about appropriate behavior for consumers of urban advice—municipal officials—are simply the converse of principles that apply to producers. These may be very briefly mentioned; others deserve more attention.

If You Don't Want Advice, Don't Ask For It. This rule would hardly be worth stating if urban officials were obliged to pay for the advice they receive. But as many of our cases (the observatories, USAC, UTS) demonstrate, federal agencies may pay most or, in effect, all of the bills. Such financial contributions as are required of the city may either be genuine but trivial, or apparently substantial but in fact the product of imaginative accounting.

As the cases (Cleveland, Los Angeles, San Francisco) demonstrate, city officials often enter consulting relationships under such circumstances even when their interest in the promised advice is weak, and when their participation in the data gathering, analysis, and testing of proposals will therefore be minimal. When that happens, the nonmonetary costs turn out to be high. At a minimum, the funders' expectations are dashed, as the USAC and CRP examples painfully demonstrate. At worst, such efforts involve distraction, diversions of staff talent when something must belatedly be salvaged from the effort, and political embarrassment. Again the USAC and CRP examples are in point.

If You Want Subordinates To Be Advised, and They Don't, Reconsider. Closely related is the observation that officials who expect to use consultants to force innovation on subordinate agencies should think twice before proceeding. As RAND's relations with New York City's Human Resources Administration and Police Department demonstrate, reluctant agencies can readily repel unwanted advisers introduced by their political superiors. They can simply decline to help advisers learn the facts, identify the problem, or understand the constraints on action. If withholding information is insufficient, the hostile agency can simply escort the unwanted adviser to the borders of some unmarked bureaucratic minefield. The explosion that follows may bloody the adviser and embarrass his sponsors, but—as RAND's New York police work shows—it is likely to leave the hostile agency unscathed.

How Much Can You Contribute? Assuming advice is wanted, the prospective client must consider what he can contribute to its production and to the harder task of inducing whatever change it proposes. The greater his capacity to help shape the advice—finding of facts, definition of problems, specification of constraints, choice of solutions—and the larger his ability to initiate and manage the processes of change, the less the client need expect from his adviser. The less he can contribute, the more he must expect. The ultimate rule remains: between them, client and adviser should have in hand or in prospect whatever intellectual, managerial, financial, and political resources that innovation is likely to require. To the degree they do not, the resulting advice is likely to be unusable.

Know the Producer; Learn the Product. A recent study examined each of the several dozen U.S. cases in which consultants used formal analytic models to help develop proposals for improvement in municipal police and correction agencies. The study concluded that in every case where the consultants had a useful impact, three conditions were met: the client department understood at the beginning of the work roughly what the analysis would be able to show and what it would not; the department understood at the beginning the time and effort likely to be required before the model became reliable enough to be useful; and strong personal relationships developed between the analysts and important departmental officials.[6]

Though the evidence from advice relationships having other purposes is less clear-cut, it is similar. Clients who are not in the hands of a selfless provider of "intensive care" may have to contribute patience and encouragement as well as effort. That is far easier if client and adviser have formed relations of personal confidence, and the client has understood from the beginning the potential difficulties as well as the promise of the analysis being performed for him.

Let Him Borrow the Watch. "A consultant is someone who borrows your watch to tell you the time, and then keeps the watch." So goes the familiar complaint. But watch borrowing is inevitable and proper; the adviser needs to know what his client thinks the problem is and what he believes the solution will be. A capable and serious adviser will find more than one way to tell time, but he has good reason to report his findings to the client in familiar terms. Recall the injunctions to advisers to avoid originality and to encourage their clients to regard the solutions proposed as their own.

In many cases, the client may be wholly justified in taking proprietary pride in a proposal: the adviser has told him little or nothing he did not previously know. Yet the adviser may still have been useful. He may have lent the prestige of independent expertise to a proposal that needed such reinforcement. He may also have assembled the first authoritative evidence that the client was right. In municipal systems resistant to change, where high confidence that an innovation will work may be an absolute prerequisite to movement, that is a substantial contribution. Recall that New York City's fire chief "knew" that dispatching fewer units to some types of first alarms than to others made sense. But he also knew that the first time lives were lost or great damage was done at a fire to which a small first response was sent, he and the mayor would be attacked by a neighborhood or ethnic group, a city councilman, or a fireman's union. In those circumstances, it was comforting to have his answer already in hand: sophisticated analysis had shown that the new system produced more than offsetting savings of life and property, and a prestigious adviser had independently verified the department's judgment that the new procedure was effective. Vera's bail experiment and RAND's rent control studies had the same effect.

Devise an Experiment.   Most consultants and most clients assume that advice has its greatest effect when formally delivered or released to the press. As to some problems, however, leverage may be small then and smaller thereafter. This will be especially true when, as is common, the relevant bureaucracy is not actively hostile to a proposal but is skeptical that it will work. After the consultant has departed, that skepticism, coupled with the normal inertia of public agencies, will be sufficient to preclude movement unless the agency head or mayor devotes great effort and persistence (or substantial horse trading) to getting the proposal adopted.

In such a case, the best strategy is probably not to await a final recommendation but to run an experiment. The advantages are several. Only a small portion of the department need be involved (one sanitation district out of sixty-four in the Stony Brook case). The adviser is still present to supply some of the entrepreneurial and administrative energy the experiment requires (as was Vera in the bail case). The anxieties of the affected agency are diminished by the understanding that if the new procedure fails, it will be modified or dropped. The care taken by the adviser in preparing his proposal is enhanced by his knowledge that it will be tried while he is still fully, perhaps publicly, associated with it. The experiment will almost certainly show how modifications in the proposal will in fact improve it or make it more acceptable. A successful trial will rebut the presumption that consultants (especially academics) understand theory but not practice. Perhaps most important, a successful experiment will create internal advocates for the innovation. At least some of the fire or sanitation or police officials who participate in the test and become associated with its success will come to regard it as their own. They will vouch for it. Some may help lobby for its wider circulation.

Keep Them at It.   Deep knowledge of a city agency's operations and of its "culture"; an understanding of the political and bureaucratic barriers to change, strong personal relationships with officials at many levels—the cases show that these are invaluable attributes for advisers, almost preconditions to advice that produces change. The Vera, Stony Brook, Denver Observatory, EDC, and RAND-fire department cases all demonstrate what can be done when these attributes are present. Virtually every other history recounted here suggests what tends to occur without them. But these attributes require the adviser's continued contact with the client's affairs; they develop only through extended experience. Yet most consulting relationships entered by local agencies are short, ad hoc, and unrepeated or highly intermittent. They rarely allow these levels of understanding to develop. And even when such understanding is acquired, it is likely to be lost when a contract expires or a particular project is completed.

The pattern of short, specific contractual relations is probably adequate where the problems on which advice is needed are simple and well specified or where the client can institute whatever change is proposed without assistance. The pattern can also be functional where the consultant is used as a lightning rod—to absorb the opposition to an "extreme" proposal and thus make easier the acceptance of more limited change. In the first case, no enduring relation between client and consultant is needed; in the second, the adviser's disposability is a virtue. But these cases are exceptional; in most others advisers addressing complex and important issues ought, if possible, to be brought into a longer-term relationship with their client.

When the advisers can largely support themselves (Vera, Stony Brook, EDC), that conclusion is easy for local officials to observe. When advisers have to be paid, it is virtually impossible for any but the largest and wealthiest jurisdictions to follow. It may therefore be a more appropriate injunction for third-party funders than for clients.

ON DEALING WITH UNIVERSITIES

There is a special set of lessons for consumers considering the use of academics as advisers.

The Advertised Shortcomings Are Real. The shortcomings of academics as advisers which chapter 3 details are, in general, real, deep-seated, and important. Principally, academics are oriented toward teaching and research, not advice giving. Many see consulting arrangements as opportunities for publishable research or the support of graduate students. Few understand the often difficult conditions under which advice is most likely to prove useful. Fewer still are equipped to meet those conditions. The Tulsa, Pittsburgh, San Francisco, and USAC cases reflect those facts (which are neither surprising nor reprehensible). If the funds for consulting are controlled by academic administrators rather than by scholars, they are likely to support the neediest faculty, as the Cleveland and Pittsburgh cases suggest, rather than the most able. And even where capable and serious academics work well on a consulting assignment, they may have lost interest, gone on sabbatical, or become overcommitted to other obligations just when additional help is needed with implementation.

But One Can Choose. Those are important limitations. But they apply in sharply differing degree across the varied landscape of American higher education. And one can choose advisers from those elements of the university community least likely to suffer those disabilities.

Which are they? They are not defined, it seems clear, by the nature of the university. If they were, it would probably be true that the newer, urban public universities take most seriously the challenge of advising city governments and perform it best. But we have seen little evidence of such a pattern. The performances of Pittsburgh, Cincinnati, Cleveland State, *as institu-*

tions, were poor. Stony Brook, a state-supported school located sixty miles from downtown New York, performed admirably. Indeed, some observers have commented that because urban public universities are frequently not academically distinguished, they are particularly reluctant to play serious public advisory roles. Recruiting their faculties from the graduates of more distinguished schools and taking those schools as models, they overcompensate. "They want to be more academic than the Harvards," remarked the president of one such school.[7]

The Discipline Is the Unit. The identity of the academic discipline, not of the university, is the variable that most affects the odds on receiving usable advice.

The Denver campus of the University of Colorado provides a useful illustration. In the early 1970s, Denver was becoming increasingly concerned about the familiar spectrum of urban problems: housing, transportation, pollution, ethnicity and race, economic development. The university is publicly supported, attracting a high proportion of older, mostly part-time students (many of them government employees) and is oriented largely toward graduate and career training. Yet, as a whole, the school displayed no particular interest in Denver's problems. The political scientists, as one of them noted, wanted nothing to do with local government; and as William Heiss, the director of the city's Urban Observatory, remarked: "I don't think there's any way I can get a C.U. sociologist together with the Mayor of Denver."[8] But the Graduate School of Public Affairs in Denver participated effectively in the city's Urban Observatory, and its counterparts in the University's Boulder and Colorado Springs campuses did equivalent work for their local governments—even though the Boulder and Colorado Springs communities were not regarded as troubled, and though the two older campuses were oriented almost entirely to younger, full-time undergraduates. It is not the nature of the university as a whole, but the values, interests, skills, and incentives of particular departments, schools, and centers within them that largely determine whether local officials will find them helpful.

Probably three categories of departments or schools are most promising. In the first, an academic discipline corresponds directly with a municipal function: public health, social work, education, planning, criminology. Schools or departments concerned generally with public (or corporate) decision making—public policy, public administration, and business administration—make up a second category. The third involves disciplines whose connection is simply that they accept the notion of a client, someone outside the discipline whose needs it is appropriate to serve. Law, engineering, architecture, and economics fit this category.

What these three categories have in common are constituencies and professional colleagues outside the academy. Their self-esteem does not depend wholly on the respect of fellow academics. They are free, therefore, to do other than to teach and to write.

Reward Performance.   The rule is a general one, of course, but it may apply especially to academics as advisers. While praise and thanks (as well as payment) are appropriate responses to any service well performed by anyone, they are less important to persons engaging in their normal professional activities than to those working outside the main lines of their careers. The lawyer enjoys his clients' thanks, but does not need them. The respect of his partners, associates, and other members of the bar is more important to him. But the academic adviser is little honored within the university for his work outside it, and that work may well cost him psychic bumps and bruises—as Stanley Altman commented earlier. If further such excursions are desirable, then they ought to be encouraged. Public praise for a private person is rare and correspondingly valued. For a public university, it may also help induce additional funding, thus rewarding administration as well as faculty. Acknowledging the value of an adviser's help takes little effort and may produce palpable benefits.

Lessons for Third Parties

Many of the advice relationships we have reviewed have been funded wholly or in part by third parties, principally foundations or the federal government. Given the pressures on city budgets, such funding, brokering, and encouragement from third parties is likely to continue to prove crucial. Yet the difficulties created by a third party are often crippling. It seems useful, therefore, to conclude by reviewing the lessons these histories suggest for triangular relationships.*

Small Failures Can Be Made into Big Ones. The first lesson for third-party funders is simply that they are playing a game in which losers outnumber winners. Continued unskillful play may only create additional failures or transform small failures into large ones.

We have seen that advice relationships may fail for any of many reasons—the absence on the client's side of interest in the advice, or ability to understand it, or capacity to use it; the absence on the adviser's side of professional competence, or ability to gain the client's confidence, or willingness to assist in the end game of implementation. But while failure is common, it is also generally recognized as failure by the principal parties, and the relationship quickly terminates. There is a

---

*Federal and state funders of local government are often unable, of course, to exercise much discretion in offering such support. Some programs are bound by legislated formulas or by less formal but equally pressing requirements to spread the money around. The rules offered here are of little use under such conditions. They are intended for situations in which federal or state officials are relatively free to discriminate among potential grantees on substantive grounds.

circumstance, however, in which that useful reflex fails: where external benefactors are present. Virtually the only large-scale, systematic, painfully drawn-out failures we have reviewed (the Pittsburgh and San Francisco CRPs; the Tulsa case; most of the urban observatories; and USAC) have been supported by third-party funders.

Supply Is Not the Problem.   The next lesson, an obvious one, is also the central message of the book: simply increasing the supply of "good advice" is not helpful. Often as we have repeated it, the point is worth restating here since many third-party funders have assumed the opposite. Where advice is not limited to technical issues and is meant to do more than inform, advisers of high competence and genuine expertise, whether drawn from business, from universities, or from the professional consulting community, have commonly been unable to provide it in a form that local governments could use. The larger the problem, the truer that proposition. Wholly technical issues aside, then, the main constraint on better municipal performance has not been a shortage of good ideas; it has been, and is, the political, managerial, and fiscal incapacity to put good ideas to use.

Then what can the interested third party do?

Strengthen Incentives to Innovate.   One form of useful intervention may be to strengthen the demand for innovation.

The most powerful single influence on public officials is public opinion—especially sustained and well-focused public opinion. It is not surprising, then, that few good tests of the quality of municipal services are available for the public, and that where they are available—in the form of pupil reading and mathematics scores, for example, or infant mortality rates— they often precipitate public demand for change. Such indices also serve to measure the success or failure of attempted reforms.

Third parties might therefore try to heighten demand for

change by sponsoring the development and continuous publication of measures of municipal performance. Local social and economic indicators would point to some phenomena (demographic trends, employment rates, public attitudes, crime trends) for which local government would only partially be responsible, but even these might suggest useful redirection of municipal effort. Indicators of service efficiency (mean response-time to fire and police alarms, incidence of erroneous or fraudulent welfare claims, changes in academic test scores in relation to national norms) could focus attention more directly on the effectiveness of public agencies. The development of more sophisticated measures and the collection and publication of data to feed them would be entirely appropriate functions to establish in universities.

Investigative reporting on city agencies now typically focuses on individual scandal: inspectors taking bribes; patrolmen retiring with phoney "disabilities"; managers abusing travel funds. Far less frequently reported are the systematic failures of major programs—to place their trainees in jobs, to collect trash at costs comparable to those of private haulers, or to provide effective medical care. It might be helpful, therefore, to subsidize the training of investigative municipal reporters, to equip them to assess programs as well as to spot thefts. Establishing well-publicized annual awards to reporters, editors, or publishers who focus public attention on such systemic issues might also be useful.

Correspondingly, annual awards to city employees who have shown unusual initiative or improved the quantity or quality of a city service would reinforce incentives that are now weak in large city agencies. Relatively modest grants could establish awards that, by municipal standards, would be substantial. Especially if given to middle- and lower-level employees, they might have considerable effect. Similarly, special travel funds might be offered to city officials interested in seeing how their functions were performed in cities in which the service is highly regarded. Lecturing a bureaucrat about the superiority of a sister service elsewhere will normally produce resentment and the response that his problems are unique. An unpressured visit by a well-chosen bureaucrat to the same sister service is more likely to stimulate ideas for change that he will regard as his own.

The purpose of each of these initiatives is the same: to stimulate interest in municipal performance among the public or to induce greater support for innovation among municipal employees.

Bet the Horse, Not the Race.   Tactics for inducing greater interest in innovation may or may not work, and even when they succeed, the political skill and energy to manage innovation—to set it carefully in place and insure that it works—remain essential. That skill and energy may come, as we have discussed, from a provider of "intensive care." But such providers are rare. Unless he has one in hand, a third-party funder interested in actually inducing change must look for a client for advice with the capacity to put the advice to use. That too is rare, but it is often easy to identify. Once a track record is established, it is not hard to determine whether or not a given agency is directed by a Robert Moses, a William Heiss, or a William Donaldson. Their capacity to induce innovation may have very different sources: a long-cultivated network of allies; familiarity with both the agendas of bureaucrats and the capacities of academics; or genius at motivating bureaucracies. But whatever the source, the result is a record of accomplishment.

Requiring such leadership as a precondition of support obviously raises the odds on the effective use of third-party funds. Less obviously, it may assist not only the jurisdiction chosen but those rejected. A mayor or agency head who seeks reform but lacks the political capacity to bring it about is not helped by a project which simply adds to the store of publicized innovations he is unable to achieve.

A Broker's Lot is a Useful One, and Hard. The adviser and the official belong to different cultures. The points at which they meet, therefore, are often points of misunderstanding or conflict. Where that is not the case, it is generally because an extraordinary individual has kept it from being so. The positions of those individuals differ, but their roles are essentially the same—and they are critical. Herbert Sturz was Vera's director; William Donaldson, a city manager; Arnold Meltzner, a graduate student; William Heiss, director of an urban observatory. But each served as a translator and broker between the two cultures, and each was indispensable to the success of their relationship.

It has frequently been argued that the performance of such brokers or agents of change is crucial. Less appreciated is the psychic difficulty of their positions. At the time of the American Revolution, North Carolinians described their state as "a valley of humility between two mountains of pride." The broker or agent of change is often in a similar posture—especially where the provider of advice is a university. His task is to persuade others to want what he sees as necessary; to buffer and absorb conflict; to accept blame and to refer credit to others. Few of the others understand how much such brokers do, and success requires that few understand. That is a lonely and draining business.[9]

One lesson for third parties is simply the importance of such brokers of change and the necessity to insure that in relationships they fund there are persons prepared (and equipped) to play such a role. Another is that ways of quietly recognizing and rewarding such intermediaries may have to be invented. Their positions are hard to sustain without some such encouragement.

Look for the "Intensive Carer." Whatever necessary strengths the third party cannot find (or create) on the client's side of an advice relationship and cannot rely on a broker to provide, he must look to the adviser to supply. Given the characteristic weakness of agencies of local government as consumers of advice, most effective relationships require on the adviser's part self-discipline, political sensitivity, managerial capacity, and concern for real reform. The support for such "intensive carers," it is worth noting, will often produce something better than simply greater odds on the success of a particular project. Since institutions capable of intensive care, like Vera or EDC, tend to remain concerned for long periods with the related problems of a *system*—of criminal justice, or health care, or education—continued reform in the system as a whole is made more likely. And a model is developed, or strengthened, for other advisers and clients to ponder.

Consider Creating an "Intensive Carer." Where no provider of intensive care exists and the local agency in need of help is not likely to be able to use the advice of a conventional consultant, consider trying to establish an intensive carer or to convert a more traditional adviser to that role. Consider, that is, but not with great optimism. "Carers" are hard to create for the same reason they are hard to find: ingenuity, high competence, political acuteness, and a persistent concern for the public good are qualities rarely found together, in individuals or organizations. Yet there is probably no function third-party funders of municipal improvement can more usefully pursue than the creation or support of institutions with the potential to provide such help.

Otherwise, Try Not to Fund Suppliers. Other kinds of providers of advice should not be funded directly. Plants turn to face the sun; grantees turn to face grantors. Where the grantor is not the client, the result is trouble: activities are designed (and described) primarily to please the source of income, not to help the intended beneficiary. LATS focused on what the Law Enforcement Assistance Administration wanted, CONSAD and ADL on what HUD wanted. The needs of Los Angeles, Pittsburgh, and San Francisco were not met; indeed they were given less and less serious attention.

"Fiscotropism," as we may unattractively label this unattractive phenomenon, should be made to increase the client's leverage, not to diminish it. Where possible, therefore, fund the consumer, not the supplier. Let the local government decide how it wants the money spent, and by whom, and on what. It may be useful to set limits on those judgments, but taking them out of the client's hands is harmful. It lessens the client's incentive to take responsibility for the work and obscure the adviser's sense of whom he is working for.[10]

"Generalizeability" is a Trap. F. Scott Fitzgerald commented, on the writing of fiction, that if he began with an individual he soon had a type, but if he began with a type he soon had nothing. A similar rule applies here. Third-party funders of advice (and especially federal agencies) tend to seek not merely useful truths, but useful truths of general applicability. They expect in this way to maximize the return on their investment. Consultants suffer from the same temptation—commercial firms because such findings may prove useful in other contracts, academics because the broader the principle discovered, the greater the credit accruing to the discoverer.

The intention is reasonable, but the results are poor. All communities believe themselves special, indeed unique. They want their advisers to address their particular concerns, not the problems of some category of communities to which a federal agency assigns them. The result is that where third-party funders insist on work whose results will be "generalizeable," city agencies lose interest, fail to cooperate, or flatly resist. The urban observatories illustrate the phenomenon and its results. And Fitzgerald's irony holds: solutions to the problem of a particular city do prove useful elsewhere. Many urban problems are widely shared. Good solutions, therefore, do have wide potential. And urban officials across the country are linked by a profusion of professional associations. Fire chiefs, police chiefs, budget officers, city managers, and mayors all have their own associations, most of which meet regularly on national, regional, and statewide bases, and which also publish journals. News of useful innovation is thus conveyed in the least threatening and most convincing way—by the reports of fellow professionals. Vera's bail reforms were designed to work in New York City, but analogous plans were adopted across the nation within five years. "Slippery water" was developed for New York City but within eight years had been adopted in more than ten cities. "Generalizeability" will come; don't strain for it.

The Highest Duty. It is true for all counselors, whether psychiatrists, management consultants, or advisers to local government, that their highest obligation is not to solve a particular problem or set of problems, but to produce a stronger client, a client better able to understand and manage his or her or its own problems. The weaker the client the stronger that obligation.

Agencies of local government are, in general, poorly equipped to face their shortcomings and to design and introduce measures to reduce them. And the pressures on city agencies are not likely to diminish. The greatest contribution the urban adviser can make, therefore, is to so involve, stimulate, educate, and encourage his clients as to make them less fearful of further innovation and better equipped to make it work. The greatest contribution of interested third parties is to insist that urban advisers understand that high, hard obligation, and that they attempt to meet it.

NOTES

Chapter 1

1. Emerson, Melville, and Thoreau (*Walden* has been characterized as the bible of anti-urbanism) well represent the early aesthetic and rural critics of the American city; Jefferson was its most prominent foe on political grounds. Probably the gloomiest view of urban masses in America was taken by de Tocqueville. "I look upon the size of certain American cities, and especially on the nature of their population, as a real danger which threatens the future security of the democratic republics of the new world; and I venture to predict that they will perish from this circumstance, unless the government succeeds in creating an armed force which while it remains under the control of the majority of the nation will be independent of the town population and able to repress its excesses." *Democracy in America*, vol. 1 (New York: A. A. Knopf, 1945), p. 189.

2. These arguments were associated especially with Professor Edward C. Banfield. For a succinct statement, see "A Critical View of the Urban Crisis," *Annals of the American Academy of Political and Social Science* 405 (January 1973): 7–14.

3. "The 224 metropolitan areas of the United States contained 125.3 million people in 1966, or 65% of the nation's total population.... About 15.2 million poor persons lived in those metropolitan areas, or 51% of all U.S. poor. Thus, metropolitan areas as a whole contained a less-than-proportional share of poor persons." The proportion of total population in nonmetropolitan areas, defined as being in poverty in 1966 was 21.4 percent. Anthony Downs, "Who are the Urban Poor?" Committee for Economic Development, Supplementary Paper #26, October 1968, p. 13.

4. "Improving Productivity in State and Local Government" Statement by the Research and Policy Committee of the Committee for Economic Development, March 1976. p. 13.

5. Ibid., pp. 31–34.

6. George E. Peterson, "Finance," in *The Urban Predicament*, ed. William Gorham and Nathan Glazer (Washington, D.C.: The Urban Institute, 1976), pp. 35–118.

7. CED statement, p. 37.

8. Ibid., p. 34.

9. The address is reprinted in *The University and the Urban Crisis*, ed. Howard E. Mitchell (New York: Behavioral Publications, 1974), pp. 19–27. (The quoted passage appears on p. 25.)

10. O.A. Singletary, ed., *American Universities and Colleges*, 10th ed. (Washington, D.C.: American Council on Education, 1968), p. 5.

11. Jacques Barzun, *The American University* (New York: Harper & Row, 1968), p. 12.

12. Earl F. Cheit, *The New Depression in Higher Education* (New York: McGraw-Hill, 1971).

13. Quoted in Clark Kerr, *The Uses of a University* (Cambridge: Harvard University Press, 1972), p. 4.

14. Barzun, *American University*, p. 10.

15. Clark Kerr, "New Challenges to the College and University," in *Agenda for the Nation*, ed. Kermit Gordon (Washington, D.C.: Brookings Institute, 1968), pp. 237–276.

Chapter 2

1. Grace M. Taher, ed., *University Urban Research Centers*, 2nd ed., (1971–72) (Washington, D.C.: The Urban Institute, 1971).

2. Quoted in Paul Dickson, *Think Tanks* (New York: Atheneum, 1971), p. 39.

3. *A Report to the Ford Foundation on the Five-Year Urban Affairs Program at the Johns Hopkins University, 1969–1974* (Baltimore, Md.: Center for Metropolitan Planning and Research at Johns Hopkins University, 1974).

4. *Urban Extension: A Report on Experimental Programs Assisted by the Ford Foundation* (New York: The Ford Foundation, 1966), pp. 33, 34.

5. *The Technical Record: Urban Affairs Activities Sponsored by Colleges and Universities in the Baltimore Region* (Baltimore, Md.: Regional Planning Council, 1967).

6. Frederick O'R. Hayes and John E. Rasmussen, eds., *Centers for Innovation in the Cities and States* (San Francisco: San Francisco Press, 1972), P. 382.

Interview in September 1976. Allan W. Ostar, director of the American Association of State Colleges and Universities, remarked that he " . . . could not think of any university urban center that had an outward rather than a student-education focus."

7. Robert C. Wood, "The Contribution of Political Science to Urban Form," in *Urban Life and Form*, ed. Werner Z. Hirsch (New York: Holt, Rinehart & Winston, 1963), pp. 122–126, quoted in *Evaluation of the Urban Observatory Program* (Washington, D.C.: National Academy of Public Administration, 1971), p. 7.

8. Quoted in National Academy of Public Administration, *Evaluation of the Urban Observatory Program*, p. 9.

9. Ibid., pp. 1, 2.

10. "An Evaluation of the Urban Observatory Program," (New York, Washington, D.C.: Greenleigh Associates, January 1974), p. 27.

11. All quotations concerning Cleveland are drawn from interviews, October 1976.

12. All quotations concerning Denver are drawn from interviews, December 1976.

13. Several representative titles are cited in *Integrated Municipal Information Systems: Programs and Projects of the U.S. Urban Information Systems Interagency Committee* (Washington, D.C.: Public Technology, 1975), p. 8.

14. J. Terry Edwards, "The Politics of Management in a Third Sector Organization." (Paper given at University of Kansas, Lawrence, Kans., 1976).

15. "Local Government Information Systems: A Study of USAC and the Future Application of Computer Technology" (Report of the USAC Support Panel, Assembly of Engineering, National Research Council, National Academy of Sciences, Washington, D.C., 1976), p. 23.

16. Edwards, "Politics of Management," p. 22.

17. Interview, September 1976.

18. Interview, February 1977.

19. C. J. Roberts, "The Professors of the City: Inception and Overview," in *A Case Study of the Professors of the City*, ed. Eugene F. Cates (Norman: University of Oklahoma Press, 1975), pp. 1–11.

20. Cates, *Professors of the City*, p. 29.

21. *Progress Report*, Spring 1969, Professors of the City Project, cited in Cates, *Professors of the City*, p. 75.

22. All quotations concerning Cincinnati are drawn from interviews, October 1976.

23. All quotations concerning Oakland are drawn from interviews, December 1976.

24. Conversation with the author, February 1977.

25. Jerry E. Mechling, "A Successful Innovation: Manpower Scheduling," *Journal of Urban Analysis* 2, no. 2 (1974): 259–313.

26. CRP Amended Application, October 1962, p. CR–121–21, quoted in Garry D. Brewer, *Politicians, Bureaucrats, and the Consultant: A Critique of Urban Problem Solving* (New York: Basic Books, 1973), p. 110.

27. Brewer, *Politicians, Bureaucrats, and the Consultant*, p. 196.

28. Ibid., p. 213.

29. Ibid., p. 208.

30. Ibid., p. 209.

31. Ibid., p. 209.

32. Ibid., p. 210.

Chapter 3

1. Norman Krumholz and Janice Cogger, "Social Science Research and Public Policy: Bridging the Gap" (Talk delivered at Social Science Research Symposium, Case Western Reserve University, April 24, 1976), p. 3.

2. J.R. Pease, *Public Service and the Public University: Environmental Problem-Solving and Research* (Amherst: University of Massachusetts, 1971), Ph.D. diss.

3. International City Management Association, "Science-Technology Advice to Local Governments," *Journal of the ICMA* 2–71 (November 1970): table 10, pp. 33–35.

4. William C. Pendleton, "Urban Studies and the University: The Ford Foundation Experience" (Address delivered at the New Orleans Regional Conference of the Office of Urban Affairs, American Council on Education, April 5, 1974). p. 10.

5. Max F. Millikan, "Inquiry and Policy: the Relation of Knowledge to Action," in *The Human Meaning of Social Sciences*, ed., Daniel Lerner, (New York: Merdian Books, 1959), pp. 158–180.

6. Martin Rein and Sheldon H. White, "Policy Research: Belief and Doubt" (Paper presented at a conference on "The Market for Policy Research," Vienna Roundtable, Cambridge, Mass., September 1975), pp. 40, 41.

7. Joseph Rowe, provost for engineering, Case Western Reserve University, in conversation with the author, October 1976.

8. William C. Pendleton, "University-City Relations Revisited" (Address delivered at Portland State University, February 25, 1975), pp. 6–8.

9. Nathan Caplan, Andrea Morrison, and Russell J. Stambaugh, "The Use of Social Science Knowledge in Policy Decisions at the National Level: A Report to Respondents," Institute for Social Research, University of Michigan, Ann Arbor, 1975, p. 37.

10. In a review of the history and utility of various mathematical models of the criminal justice system, Jan Chaiken and coauthors remark, " . . . it is much more interesting for an analyst to design a model from scratch than to use somebody else's. Thus it is possible to have endless cycles of reinventing the wheel without any advances being made in either the conceptual underpinnings of the model or its ease of use." "Criminal Justice Models: An Overview," *RAND Report R-1859-DOJ*, October 1975, p. 128.

11. Conversation with the author, October 1976.

12. See, for example, "Final Report of the Interstate Technology Transfer Work-

shop," Center for Local Government Technology, Oklahoma State University, December 1975, pp. 1–13; "Suggestions for an Urban Strategy for a Large Urban University," Institute for Urban Studies, Cleveland State University, July 1973, pp. 45 ff.; "Internal Obstacles to Successful Programs in Urban Affairs and Academic Public Service" (Talk by Glenn W. Fisher, Wichita State University, presented at a workshop to consider the development of a cooperative actions program in urban affairs and academic public service, January 6, 1976, and published in the proceedings of that workshop, p. 19). For similar conclusions related to relations between universities and state governments, see Gene A. Bramlett, *The Academic Community: A Backup Force to State Government*, Southern Regional Education Board, September 1974, especially pp. 110, 187 ff.

13. Ferguson, "Final Report of the Interstate Technology Transfer Workshop," p. 3.

14. Brice Ratchford, talk prepared for National Conference on Public Service and Extension in Higher Education, June 1974.

15. Glenn W. Fisher, "Internal Obstacles to Successful Programs," p. 25.

16. Robert Nathans, "The University and Approaches to Problems of State and Local Government" (Talk delivered at conference on Institutions of Higher Education as a Resource in the Solution of National Problems, May 1972, and reproduced in "A Question of Partnership," proceedings of that conference, p. 41 ff.).

17. Cleveland State University, "Suggestions for an Urban Strategy," p. 47.

Chapter 4

1. International City Management Association, "Science-Technology Advice in Local Governments," *Journal of the ICMA* 2, no. 11 (November 1970): 1–48.

2. Garry D. Brewer, *Politicians, Bureaucrats, and the Consultant* (New York: Basic Books, 1973), p. 173.

3. Ibid., p. 211. Frederick O'R. Hayes has argued that the CRP projects should be regarded not as advice to city governments but as poorly-designed federal attempts to finance state-of-the-art development of new planning techniques. (Letter from Hayes to William Pendleton, August 1979.) However that may be, the local officials involved expected something of use to them.

4. Ibid., p. 205.

5. Ibid., p. 106.

6. Ibid., p. 168.

7. Ibid., p. 116.

8. Ibid., p. 115.

9. Ibid., p. 115.

10. Ibid., p. 165. Interestingly, in its promotional literature of the early 1970s, ADL described the San Francisco CRP in these terms:

The San Francisco program is unique in comparison with other renewal plans in that it uses a mathematical simulation model . . . the computer program enables city officials and planners to determine in advance the effect of policies and programs and so enables them to choose the most feasible and beneficial policies and programs for the city . . . the final result of the study was a framework for meeting market demands for urban renewal so that the city could realize maximum efficiency from every dollar spent in community improvements.

"Qualifications in Public and Managerial Economics," Arthur D. Little, Inc. (undated), p. 2.

11. Conversation with the author, September 1976.

12. See Roger E. Levien, "Independent Public Policy Analysis Organizations: A Major Social Invention" (RAND Corporation paper, 1969), pp. 4–15.

13. The institute published over 150 reports of individual studies, as well as four comprehensive annual reports. In addition, much of the institute's history is covered in accounts appearing in Frederick O'R. Hayes and John E. Rasmussen, *Centers for Innovation in the Cities and States* (San Francisco: San Francisco Press, 1972); Paul Dickson, *Think Tanks* (New York: Atheneum, 1971); M. Greenberger, M. A. Crenson, and B. L. Crissey, *Models in the Policy Process* (New York: Russell Sage Foundation, 1976)—in which particularly detailed and perceptive analyses of the institute's work for the Health Services Administration and the fire department appear; and in an unpublished evaluation prepared for the Ford Foundation in 1971 (cited hereafter as Ford "Evaluation"). The skeptical reader may wish to rely more heavily on these accounts by observers of the institute than on the discussion here since the present author was the first president of the institute and thus shared responsibility for much of the institute's work here described.

14. Gil Bernstein, Assistant Administrator of HSA, quoted in Ford "Evaluation," p. 62.

15. Dr. Thomas Rockwell, director of RAND Bio-Medical Program, quoted in Ford "Evaluation," p. 77.

16. The dispatching study, the sources and nature of the resistance to it, and its outcome are described in detail in Greenberger et al, *Models in the Policy Process*, pp. 257–262.

17. Greenberger et al, *Models in the Policy Process*, p. 284.

18. I. S. Lowry, "Reforming Rent Control in New York City; The Role of Research in Policymaking" *Policy Sciences* 3 (1972): 47–58.

19. Ford "Evaluation," p. 45.

20. Frederick O'R. Hayes, "Researchers as Consultants." Forthcoming study of the Lindsay Administration, chap. 7.

21. Ibid.

22. From a description of LATS by its president, Edward H. Erath, in Hayes and Rasmussen, *Centers for Innovation*, p. 213.

23. An evaluation of LATS prepared for the Ford Foundation, June 1972, p. 50.

24. Ibid., p. 56.

25. Ibid., p. 29.

26. Ibid., p. 75.

27. Cited in Walter S. Baer, "University Relationships with other R & D Performers" (RAND Corporation paper, August 1976), p. 57.

28. See Baer, "University Relationships," pp. 56–57.

29. Ibid., p. 4.

30. Ibid., p. 52.

31. Nathan Caplan, Andrea Morrison, and Russel J. Stambaugh, "The Use of Social Science Knowledge in Policy Decisions at the National Level," Institute for Social Research, University of Michigan, Ann Arbor, 1975, p. 24.

32. "The Federal Investment in Knowledge of Social Problems." (The report of a Study Project on Social Research and Development, vol. 1, National Academy of Sciences, Washington, D.C., 1978), p. 18.

33. Cited in Caplan, Morrison, and Stambaugh, *Use of Social Science Knowledge*, p. 27.

34. Gene A. Bramlett, "The Academic Community: A Backup to State Govern-

ment" (A report submitted by the Southern Regional Education Board to the National Science Foundation, September 1974), pp. 165–167.

35. Robert F. Wilcox, in conversation with the author, December 1976.

36. "The Art of the Practical" (An evaluation of the Vera Institute of Justice prepared for the Ford Foundation, 1970), p. 9.

37. Conversation with the author, October 1976.

38. David Rogers, *Can Business Management Save the Cities?* (New York: The Free Press, 1978), p. 64.

39. Ibid., p. 78.

40. Ibid., p. 157.

41. Conversation with the author, November 1976.

Chapter 5

1. Robert Fichter, in conversation with the author, February 1977.

2. Peter L. Szanton, "Systems Problems in the City," *Operations Research*, 20, no. 3 (May–June 1972): 469.

3. Charles Darwin, quoted in Charles P. Curtis, *A Commonplace Book* (New York: Simon & Schuster, 1957), p. 24.

4. Conversation with the author, November 1967.

5. Conversation with the author, October 1976.

6. J. Chaiken et al., "Criminal Justice Models: An Overview," RAND Report R-1859-DOJ, October 1975, pp. 123–4.

7. Warren Bennis, president of the University of Cincinnati, in conversation with the author, October 1976.

8. Conversation with the author, December 1976.

9. The author questioned eight such intermediaries about the psychic difficulties of their jobs. The intermediaries commonly expressed gratitude that an outsider understood the relative selflessness of their work, controlled resentment that others did not and an unwillingness to remain indefinitely in such a position.

10. Interestingly, Caplan and coauthors found that of the social science information used directly in policy making by federal agencies, 51 percent had been produced in-house, and 35 percent had been produced externally on agency contract. Therefore, 86 percent was self-funded. Since it is hardly likely that 86 percent of all relevant and available data were self-funded, the figures suggest the degree to which government officials give differential attention to the research product for which they feel some responsibility. Nathan Caplan, Andrea Morrison, and Russel J. Stambaugh, "The Use of Social Science Knowledge in Policy Decisions at the National Level," Institute for Social Research, University of Michigan, Ann Arbor, 1975, p. 8.

INDEX

Academics, 39–41, 140–44; *see also* Universities
ADL: *see* Arthur D. Little
Aerospace industry, 105
Agricultural and mechanical colleges, 11
Agricultural experiment stations, 9
Air pollution abatement, 99
Albuquerque, N.M., 22, 24, 25n
Altman, Stanley, 141, 152
Ambulance services, 31
American Society for Public Administration, 44
Analects, The, 3
Ann Arbor, Mi., 14n
Arthur D. Little (ADL), 76–80, 107, 159, 164n10
Atlanta, Ga., 22

Bail reform, 116–18, 148, 160
Bales, Carter, 99–100
Baltimore, Md., 20, 22, 24
Barzun, Jacques, 13
Battelle Institute, 127
Beame, Abraham, 96–97
Bennis, Warren, 9, 41–43, 63
Berkeley, 14, 14n; *see also* University of California at Berkeley
Bismarck, Otto von, 57n
Black population, 4–5, 19
Boeing Corporation, 127

Booz, Allen and Hamilton, 74
Boston, Ma., 22, 24, 25n, 129n
Boy's Life, 116
Bramlett, Gene A., 68n
Brewer, Garry D., 51n, 54, 75, 77, 141
Bridgeport, Conn., 25n
Brookhaven Laboratories, 48n
Budget Bureau of New York City, 48, 80–85, 87, 90–91, 94, 100–1, 119, 135
Business schools, 108

Cambridge, Ma., 14n
Can Business Management Save the Cities?, 120n
Caplan, Nathan, 62
Carnegie Corporation, 12
Case Western Reserve, 26, 65
Center for Regional Economic Studies (CRES), 52–54
Chaiken, Jan, 163n10
Champion, George, 120
Charlotte, N.C., 31
Chase Manhattan Bank, 120
Children of Light and the Children of Darkness, The, 17
Cincinnati, Ohio, 41–44, 126, 142–43, 150
City governments: assessment of university-based advice to, 57–

Index